Sherri,

Infusion

90 DAILY DOSES OF WISDOM, TRUTH AND ENCOURAGEMENT

Thanks for you love

Boyd Bailey

WISDOM HUNTERS

For Jesus Christ glory

Proverbs 13:20

Published in Roswell, Georgia, by Wisdom Hunters, LLC.

Scripture taken from the Holy Bible, New International Version®, NIV®, Copyright © 1973, 1978, 1984 by International Bible Society. Used by Permission of Zondervan. All rights reserved.

Cover Design by Sprocket, Inc. (www.SprocketCreative.com)

Wisdom Hunters, LLC.
1080 Holcomb Bridge Road
Building 200, Suite 140
Roswell, GA 30076
Visit us at www.WisdomHunters.com

The Wisdom Hunters name and logo are trademarks of Wisdom Hunters, LLC.

Printed in the United States of America

First Wisdom Hunters printing: August 2006

ISBN: 0-9788042-0-1

Dedication

To my wife, lover and best friend, Rita.

Thank you for your wisdom and for asking me the hard questions.

Contents

Acknowledgements

Thanks to my ethics professor in graduate school, who said in passing one day, "You have a gift for writing and you should develop it."

Thanks to Andy Stanley, who allowed me to practice writing on various projects and for saying early in our friendship that the way to learn to write, is to write.

Thanks to Mom, who writes well and inspires me to do the same.

Thanks to Lanny Donoho, who paved the way for me with his engaging God's Blogs.

Thanks to Lee McCutchan, who faithfully edits the daily e-mail, "Wisdom Hunters...Right Thinking."

Thanks to Karen Williams for your valued consulting and resourcefulness around book cover design, edits, formatting, publishing and printing.

Thanks to my editor, Jim Armstrong, for your unwavering excellence.

Thanks to Richard Shupert and Joe Schlosser for driving the marketing, sales and distribution.

Thanks to Scott Melby and David Deeter for underwriting the majority of the book costs.

Thanks to mentors over the years who have modeled daily time with Christ.

Thanks to John Woodall, who encouraged me to remain faithful and useable for the Lord.

Thanks to Charlie and Patty Renfroe, who have been relentless in their radical friendship.

Thanks to Ministry Ventures and Wisdom Hunters for allowing me to serve.

Thanks to friends and acquaintances who, through their authentic living, have allowed me to walk with them up close and personal, doing life together.

Thanks to the Lord for His work of grace through the power of His Spirit and His Word!

Introduction

The definition of *infusion* is…

> *n* 1: the act of infusing, imbuing, or pouring in: ***instilling***
> 2: the process of ***extracting*** certain active properties by
> steeping or soaking 3: the operation of ***introducing*** saline
> or other solutions into the veins.[1]

The purpose of this book is to compel you into a regular time with
God so that, as a result, you will apply His wisdom to your life. The goal
of this infusion process is for you to ***instill*** perspective into your life,
extract sin from your life, and ***introduce*** truth into your life. Freedom in
Christ balanced with fear of God is wise living for the follower of Jesus.
But for this to happen, there has to be intentionality on your part.
Spiritual exercise is like physical exercise. Prayer prepares your heart, and
Scripture prepares your mind. Prayer and Scripture infused together
become wisdom. This process of regular spiritual infusion gives you the
emotional and mental stamina to "walk wisely" within a world of hurt. It
is the power of renewing your mind that Paul talks about in Romans
chapter 12.

Tom Babcock taught me this right after my conversion to Christ,
during my freshman year of college. Tom, a pharmacist in our small town
in north Alabama, stressed the daily importance of "exhaling"—confessing my sins—and "inhaling"—drawing on the influence of the Holy
Spirit. We prayed together, shared Christ together, and studied the Bible
together. Tom was insistent on the discipline of daily time in God's Word
and in prayer. So, from the very beginning of my walk with Christ, spiritual disciplines were incorporated into my life. They were infused without
me knowing it. I was ignorance on fire, but I had sense enough to know
what I didn't know. I was a disciplined person by nature, so what Tom
modeled for me resonated as reality. This proved to be a firm foundation
on which to build a life of following Christ, albeit more through failures
than successes. It has been in times of failure that I have grown the most:
too much work, too little rest. Busyness crowding out time with my heavenly Father was a consequence of my service for God replacing my intimacy with God. My biggest struggle has been replacing anger with
forgiveness. Unresolved hurt, I am learning, leads to anger.

So after 26 years of walking, falling and sometimes stumbling along with Jesus, I still need daily infusions from Him. Infusions of patience, infusions of humility, infusions of grace, infusions of courage, infusions of hope, infusions of contentment, infusions of character, infusions of holiness, infusions of forgiveness and infusions of love, just to name a few.

These writings originated "real time" out of my regular reading of the Daily Walk Bible, since Gayle Jackson challenged our "Wisdom Hunters Roundtable" group in the fall of 2004 to be so immersed in the Scripture that "the Word of God" was on our breath. Thanks, Gayle, for motivating and mentoring me toward this end.

I pray that regular infusions from the Lord become a habit of your life. There is nothing more fulfilling and rewarding than walking wisely with Christ and with others seeking to do the same. I pray *Infusion* will facilitate your faith into wise thinking and wise living. Enjoy!

In Christ,

Boyd Bailey

Wisdom Hunters, LLC

---

1. *New Illustrated Webster's Dictionary of the English Language*, New York: PMC Publishing Company, 1994 printing, p. 499.

Infusion

Risky Request

"The Lord said to Abram, 'Leave your country, your people and your father's household and go to the land I will show you.'"
Genesis 12:1

Sometimes God asks you to take a risk. Sometimes His requests seem to carry tremendous risk. He may ask you to leave a job. All these years you have labored faithfully in a specific role, and now it appears that He is directing you to a totally different work environment. This is something to take to heart. It is a big deal. It is important that you provide for your family and, yes, you have been effective in your work. But, if God is calling you to this new endeavor, then it is His responsibility to give you the wisdom and ability to carry out His adventurous assignment.

It is normal to be nervous. It is normal to be apprehensive. But, take comfort that God does not lead you to a place where He does not provide for you. Of course His provision may appear to be different than it appeared in the past; nevertheless, He is faithful to those who are obedient to His call. God's call cannot be ignored. He is consistent and clear when He calls you to an opportunity filled with uncertainty. Let faith be your guide. Ambiguity can be an asset because it causes you to depend on God. Do not allow fear to cloud your convictions. If He is asking you to get out of the boat, then He will provide an acrylic floor on the water. Great faith accompanies bold obedience. Dance with the one who brought you. Faith has sustained you thus far, and faith will sustain you going forward. Great results normally follow great risk. However, a Holy Spirit-led risk is really no risk at all. God says it, so that settles it.

Still, responding to and implementing the Lord's bold request can be hard. It is hard to leave family and friends. It is hard to leave the best church in the world. It is hard to leave a familiar environment for one filled with ambivalence and contingency. So, it is OK to struggle with the difficulty of transition. But, do not allow the difficulty to prolong your procrastination. Begin preparing today, so that you can respond to Christ's call tomorrow.

Indeed, following God's risky request does not preclude planning. Planning is your friend. Planning is responsible and spiritual. Planning does not exclude faith; rather, it enhances faith. Your faith is more robust when you have a Holy Spirit-crafted plan. So, be careful not to presume on God and become irresponsi-

---

"He who walks with the wise grows wise, but a companion of fools suffers harm." Proverbs 13:20

Dose 1

ble through lack of planning. Surround yourself with trusted advisors who can coach you through the planning process. God can bless a mess, but normally He blesses a prayerful plan.

It may take a year or two of intentional planning to be prepared to "pull the trigger" on God's new and exciting call on your life, but the process of preparation and planning is well worth it. You will learn a lot about yourself and God during this time. Money will become less important and people will become more important. Your security will flow from your Savior and not from stuff. Your intimacy with your spouse and heavenly Father will go deeper and wider than any other time in the past. God's risky request is for your best. Because of your obedience, the Kingdom of God will be much better. Heaven's population will increase because you have decreased. Continue to go with God. Following Christ is really no risk at all!

God's Part

Though it may appear risky to our limited vision, God's call is sure, and God's provision is unlimited—He makes it happen.

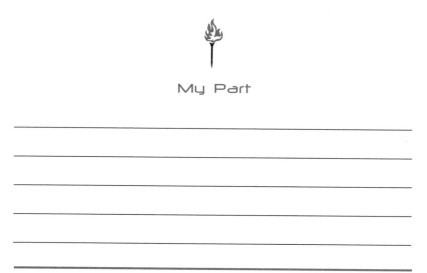

My Part

_____

_____

_____

_____

_____

A Father's Influence

"Then the father realized this was the exact time at which Jesus had said to him, 'Your son will live.' So he and all his household believed."
John 4:53

A father's influence is larger than life. Your behavior casts a shadow that affects your family in the here and now. This is God's design. Someone has to ultimately be responsible, and it is the father. You may very well be married to someone smarter and more spiritual than you. Certainly she is easier on the eyes than you! Regardless of all her positive qualities, the buck still stops with the father. What you do influences. What you don't do influences. What you say influences. What you don't say influences. Either way your actions do speak louder than your words.

However, do not let the pressure of your responsibility to provide a positive influence overwhelm you. You are a man. You like challenges. You do not have to be alone as you attempt to exert wise influence. Partner with Jesus! Let the peace of Christ reign in your heart. Then you will become a stabilizing influence in your family. Allow God to love you thoroughly so that you can do the same with your family. It takes being loved to love.

Here is the secret of a father's influence: Become a student of your heavenly Father. Become intimate with Him as His son. As you learn His ways and motivations, emulate them. He is your model. He is your example. He is your hope. Moreover, flee from the "victim" mindset that blames bad habits on your dad. Your dad did what he could with what he had. You know better. You cannot control your dad, but you can change for the better.

Do not be lazy in your living by defaulting to bad habits that were modeled for you. Sometimes a wrong example is more compelling than a right example. The crippling consequence of bad behavior compels you to avoid the same. Your child has an opportunity to exceed his or her grandfather in commitment and character. Your influence is a facilitator for their wise living. Influence is assumed with your small children, and it is earned with your teens and adult children. Influence your family relationally and you win. Influence your family by ultimatums and you lose. Show them Christ-like living first, and then you earn the right to influence them effectively.

"He who walks with the wise grows wise, but a companion of fools suffers harm." Proverbs 13:20

Dose 2

Your "coffee and Christ" time in the morning may be your highest leveraged influence. Your love for Jesus promotes their love for Jesus. The more your child and wife fall in love with Jesus, the more they will experience God's best. The more they experience God's best, the more they influence their circle of relationships for Christ. It is an expanding circle. Thus, you leverage your influence way beyond your family. This is God's plan.

Influence for God starts with the father. The man of the household is the spiritual leader. Your responsibility extends way beyond bringing home the bacon. Most anybody can do that. First and foremost, God has called you to influence your home with His grace and truth. As the father goes, so goes the home. They will want your Jesus as they see Jesus in you. It is scary and humbling at the same time. Your godly influence is a matchless gift to your family. It is a gift that keeps on giving. Be an influencer motivated by love for God and people. Hang out with your heavenly Father so that you can be the most effective earthly father. There are no silver bullets—just Jesus. He is your influencer so that you can influence your family on His behalf. This is a father's best influence!

God's Part

Jesus will multiply your influence on His behalf.

My Part

_____

_____

_____

_____

_____

Morning Preparation

"In the morning, O Lord, you hear my voice; in the morning I lay my requests before you and wait in expectation."
Psalm 5:3

Start the day with God. This is your best preparation. This is the best part of the day because it is the beginning of the day. Appointments have yet to assault your calendar. Interruptions are blockaded from your schedule. Each day is a new day full of opportunity, challenge and problems. Because each day is unique, we need a daily dose of God. We need His wisdom, forgiveness and perspective. Just as our body needs exercising and bathing; so our mind, soul and heart need God's cleansing and renewal. Time with God feeds our soul like a nice meal nourishes our body. A malnourished soul will lead to a sick life. You can fast from God, but this is not a healthy fast.

Your fasting from God may be as result of moving too quickly. Slow down your pace or He may slow it down for you. Assuming you have rested well the night before, your mind and body are the most receptive in the morning. Therefore, it makes sense to use this pliable time of the day to recalibrate with God. First in, first out is a good description of what happens in the morning. If the worries of the world consume our beginning of the day, then worry will come out first during the day. If trust in God fills our day's beginning, then trust will come out first during the day.

Jesus modeled this for us as He rose before the day began to spend time quietly with His heavenly Father. You may need to find a quiet spot with the fewest distractions so that you can listen intently to your heavenly Father. Wake up with God while the world sleeps. Then, when the world awakes, you can greet it with grace and truth.

Your time with God need not be complicated. Converse just as you do daily with certain friends; keep the dialogue honest and open. God already knows our heart, but we forget and we need a reminder. My heart deceives me, but God cuts through the deception and gets to the core of the matter. My anger may cause me to sin by not letting go of a person or a situation. Sometimes it is hard to let go and trust God with the matter.

You cannot blame another for your bad attitude; this is between you and God. Ask Him to do an attitude check and to fill your "gratitude tank" before

Dose 3

you run out of gas. If gratitude is not motivating your living, you will burn through energy like dried out firewood on a blistering cold winter night. Without daily doses of divine gratitude, your enthusiasm will be sucked away like smoke up a chimney. The morning is an ideal time to lay our requests before our heavenly Father. These can be requests that flow from the desires of our heart.

When you walk close with God, the desires of your heart will align more closely with His wishes for your life. This is reassuring. As you walk with Jesus each day, ask Him by faith for a pure heart. Request from Him the right spouse and a new career opportunity in His timing. Look to Him for courage to walk away from a relationship or a deal, or request that same courage from Him to accept a new challenge—one that forces you out of your comfort zone. Ask Him for the trust and the patience to accept His timing with all of the issues that are crowding your mind. There is no better way to start your day than with God!

God's Part

God always stands ready to converse with you, His child, and there is no better time for that conversation than first thing every morning.

My Part

_____

_____

_____

_____

_____

Nothing Withheld

"The angel of the Lord called to Abraham from heaven a second time and said, 'I swear by myself, declares the Lord, that because you have done this and have not withheld your son, your only son, I will surely bless you....'"
Genesis 22:15-17a

God blesses an open hand. Complete and total obedience is what He desires. There can be nothing we possess that is too sacred to give up or to give over to God. It may be a child. It may be a career. It may be an employee. It may be a relationship. It may be a habit. It may be a hurt. It may be a boat, car or house. When we surrendered to the lordship of Christ, we gave over everything to Him. It was not a matter of degrees or incremental obedience. It was total and complete submission to God with nothing withheld. Indeed, if we do hold back, He holds back. God will not fully bless partial obedience. This is not His style or expectation. His intention is to have all of you. This includes your family, finances, friends and faith. Just because you are willing to give up or give away something does not mean God will require you to do so. But, He does expect you to be willing. He looks beyond your words to your heart. It is not a begrudging giving up that He expects. Rather, He looks for you to let loose and walk away with no strings attached. He wants to bring you to the place of total contentment in Him.

He wants you to be completely and absolutely abandoned to Christ. If all you are left with is Jesus, this is enough. As long as you require Jesus plus something else, you still operate with a conditional commitment to Christ. Jesus does not need any additional help. It is Christ and Christ alone that is sufficient for the abundant life. Moreover, God's leading may be full of uncertainty, but one thing you can be certain of is His provision—in the right way at the right time. When you give up something, He replaces your sacrifice with His best.

God is not shabby in what He gives you in exchange for your not holding back anything. God releases His best when you withhold nothing. Sometimes His timing gets right down to the point of death before He intercedes on your behalf. Your vision may be on the brink of death, and this may be the very time God breathes His breath of life into it. You had to travel down this road of placing your vision in God's intensive care unit. By going with Him to the point of death with your vision, you are more committed than ever. Your faith is more robust. Your intimacy with Christ grew deeper, because you placed your vision on His altar of sacrifice. If it died, it died. This was God's call. You were willing

Dose 4

to walk away if this was the will of the Lord. But He observed your sincere faith and complete trust in Him. And because you were willing to die to the vision, He has taken your vision to a whole other level beyond your dreams. When a vision is a God-sized vision, it cannot be contained by human reason or resources. However, we have to let loose of its grip and allow God to let it explode into eternity. Grasping and withholding limits God's blessing.

Lastly, He may be calling you to lay at His altar of sacrifice a relationship. You have held on too long, and He expects you to die to the need for this person. They have controlled you, instead of the Holy Spirit. Indeed, what God expects has taken back seat to the expectations of this person. It has become a dysfunctional and divisive relationship. He may be asking you to give it up, and to give over to Him your fears. This relationship has hindered, not enhanced, your relationship with Jesus. It is not worth the energy and effort to make it work. Give it to God. Place it on His altar, and trust Him with the results. He will provide a richer and more meaningful relationship, but it starts with allowing this one to die. Deep life with Christ comes from a death. It required His death. It requires our death to self and, if necessary, the willingness for dreams and relationships to die. Withhold nothing!

God's Part

As God observes your expression of obedience through holding everything with an open hand, He takes from you what is good and puts in its place what is best.

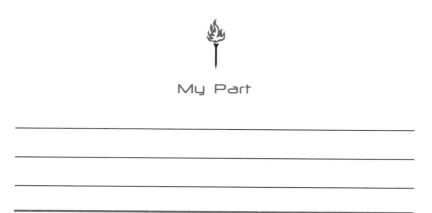

My Part

_____

_____

_____

Loyalty During Adversity

"You are those who stood by me in my trials."
Luke 22:28

It is easier to walk away from someone undergoing a time of trial than it is to stay. You are tempted to flee because so much is at risk. If you stay with them you may lose time, money and energy. There is a cost to loyalty. Therefore, because of fear, hurt and disappointment, you may choose the other road of self-preservation.

Indeed, it is hard to stay loyal to people during their time of trial. Life gets messy during adversity. Circumstances grow complex and overwhelming. The care-free life you had hoped for is out the window over night. By the way, Jesus does not promise a life without trouble.

On the contrary, as you live counter to the culture, you will encounter friction and problems. Moreover, people will make stupid choices that adversely affect you and your family. Life is not designed for limited suffering. Life is an opportunity to meet God in your suffering. So, as others suffer, you suffer. Suffering is an invitation to face your fears and embrace Christ. It is not a time to flee from your responsibilities. Adversity is a time to hunker down with God and with those who really care. It may seem like there is no hope. However, you know in your heart that there is always hope in Christ.

Yes, you may have the right to walk away from your friend in need, but having the right does not make it right. The real question is, "What is the wise thing to do?" What is wise for you? What is wise for your friend in need? What is wise for your family? What is wise for the Kingdom of God? Extract out the emotion and do the wise thing. Avoid revenge—that's for God to handle. You can stay loyal because God has done the same for you.

Christ is the ultimate loyalist. He stays loyal to you during the most difficult of times. He has stood by you when the "fair weather" friends have fled. Jesus is a rock during the gale force winds of adversity. His commitment is critical to your perseverance. Some days the only reason you are able to move forward is because of Jesus. Therefore, especially stay loyal to Jesus during this time of upheaval. Walk with Him. Do not run ahead in fear or lag behind in disappointment. Stay true to your Lord. He is there for you. He is loyal to you. He believes in you. You can do the same because He lives in you by faith. The loyalty of

"He who walks with the wise grows wise, but a companion of fools suffers harm." Proverbs 13:20

Dose 5

Christ indwells your being. You can apply a higher standard of loyalty because of the capacity Christ has given you. Jesus stands by you during the thick and the thin. You can do the same for your friends in adversity. Stay true to them because Jesus is true to you. Stay true to them because God has not given up on them.

Your suffering is your ministry. God has uniquely positioned you to care for others who are walking a similar road. Your perseverance under fire is a rock-solid foundation of faith. Many, many others will be helped and encouraged because you chose to stay loyal to your friend during a time of trial and tribulation.

Loyalty in adversity is a life preserver. It preserves the giver and it preserves the receiver. Stay loyal; loyalty begets loyalty. This is a test of loyalty. By God's grace and forgiveness, you will exceed expectations. Stay true to God and stay true to your friend during this time of adversity. Your loyalty will draw you and others closer to Jesus. Be loyal because He is loyal!

God's Part

God is fiercely loyal to His own, and He expects the same among His children.

My Part

_____

_____

_____

_____

_____

Divine Defense

"You have upheld my right and my cause; you have sat on your throne, judging righteously."
Psalm 9:4

God is our ultimate defense. This does not mean we are not involved in defending worthy causes. It is good to defend nation and family. Effective leaders defend their mission and their business model. Excellent athletic teams defend their goal from the opponent. An explosive offense will strategize in vain without the support of an aggressive defense. Successful defense attorneys are paid a lot of money because they keep their clients from serving time in prison. They are the experts that understand the law and its implications.

Orphans and widows need defending. The helpless are vulnerable in need of defense. Those of us who are followers of Jesus Christ are called not to stand idle but to stand in the gap for those who cannot defend themselves. We are advocates for the poor and needy. Your friends who have been mistreated, misunderstood or maligned behind their backs need you to step up on their behalf. You are their defender because you know their character. You know the facts of the situation and that the accusation does not line up with reality. So, it is appropriate for you to risk your safe position and to defend your friends in the face of their accusers.

Do not back down from defending truth. God's Word is truth and, yes, it can stand on its own. But we are called to be educated—not ignorant—defenders of His Word. Be so familiar with God's Word that in the face of heresy you can confidently say, "Here I stand, I can do no other." But, after all is said and done, God is our ultimate defender. There are some situations where our defense is woefully lacking, but He more than fills in the gaps.

You cannot defend your reputation, but God can. People, because of misinformation or malice, may misdiagnose who you are and what you stand for. This is out of your control. You can go through a very professional and prayerful process of letting an employee go, and that employee may still erupt in disappointment and lash back at you. Even with generous severance terms, they may gossip about you and spread rumors. It is futile to chase down a rumor. You must maintain your trust in God and do not lower yourself to attack this individual. They are in God's hands, which is exactly where you want them. Don't take matters into your own hands. You cannot handle that type of pressure and

"He who walks with the wise grows wise, but a companion of fools suffers harm." Proverbs 13:20

Dose 6

responsibility. God is your defense. Since He manages the universe, He can handle this situation. He will defend you in ways you could never conceive. The truth will persevere and, left unattended, lies will slowly die off. Like ignoring a child's temper tantrum they will eventually stop from lack of attention.

You cannot defend your motives, but God can. Over time God will use your generosity, humility and consistency to validate your motives. There will be those who question your motives because of their own struggle with impure motives. But there is no need to default to insecurity; trust God to defend you.

Cynics and naysayers have a skewed perspective. It is hard for them to accept authentic motives because they have been burned in the past. Do not debate your motives with them; let God defend you. A prayerful, patient and personal process eventually will answer many of the questions. God is our advocate. Let go of those things beyond your control, and trust Him with the results. He is the righteous judge!

God's Part

On behalf of His children, God is both defender and righteous judge. He will never fail.

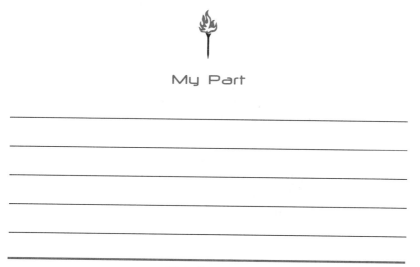

My Part

_____

_____

_____

_____

_____

Love's Commitment

*"So Jacob served seven years to get Rachel, but they seemed like only
a few days to him because of his love for her."*
Genesis 29:20

Love is committed. During the good times love is committed. During
the bad times love is committed. In some ways love is blind. It is blind to giving
up. It is blind to leaving the one it loves. It is blind to the intensity of work
required to serve the relationship. Love is a powerful, powerful force. It can make
grown men cry and cause undisciplined men to become focused. It can break a
heart or mend a heart. However, when all is said and done, love remains committed.

With love, there is no waffling back and forth. You remain loyal when you
love. The rules may change, but you still love. Adversity may be hovering over
your family, but you still love. Finances may be tight, even nonexistent, but you
still love. Your spouse's body may be deteriorating before your very eyes because
of a vicious illness, but you still love. In fact, the hounds of hell may actually
cause your love to compound during difficulty. It is during distress that you have
the opportunity for your love to shine through your service to your spouse.

Now is the time to stop whining, grumbling, complaining and feeling sorry
for your unjust circumstances. Instead, now is the time to "circle the wagons"
and ratchet up your love quotient. Greater sin requires greater love. Greater hurt
requires greater love. Greater challenge requires greater love. Greater work
requires greater love.

Moreover, untested love can be sentimental and emotionally dependent.
However, when love meets a challenge, it is galvanized and it grows. Now is the
time for your love to go deep with one another. Do not allow adversity to drive
you apart. Instead, apply the glue of love. Let love bind your hearts together. Let
the love of Christ reign supremely in and through you!

You may not have experienced unconditional love growing up or even as an
adult. Your examples may have been self-serving and conditional lovers, but now
Jesus has invaded your life and set up shop. His love machine cranks out unconditional and selfless love. Now your model for loving others is Jesus. Now you
can love your wife like Christ loves the church. You can. You must. Indeed,
loving comes more naturally for the woman than the man. This is God's design.

Dose 7

However, in Christ you have the capacity to out-love your wife. This is a stretch, but it is certainly possible. Yes, she may be hard to understand, but love her even more. Yes, she "ticks you off" sometimes, but love her even more. Yes, she is emotional and needy, but love her even more.

Love is a two-way street, but you are only responsible for driving your car of love. So, continue to steer your love toward the bride of your youth. Do not let the cares of this world callous your heart. You married a great woman, much better than you probably deserved. Set your expectations heavenward, and love with a heavenly commitment. Love covers a multitude of sins.

Grudges kill love; grace revitalizes love. Woo your woman with a commitment of love that won't quit. Then watch love accomplish God's purposes way beyond your capabilities. People are watching how you love your wife, especially current and future son-in-laws. You have to love that!

God's Part

Jesus displays love's commitment through the way He loves the church: fully, unselfishly, and sacrificially.

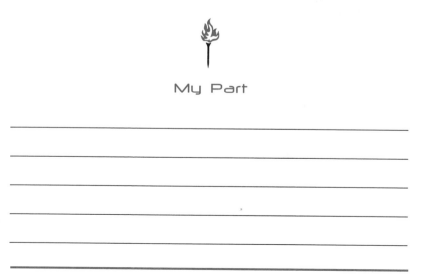

My Part

_____

_____

_____

_____

_____

Cautious Commitments

*"But Jesus would not entrust himself to them, for he knew all men. He did
not need man's testimony about man, for he knew what was in a man."*
John 2:24-25

Unwise commitments can be your downfall or, at the very
least, a distraction. It is smart to take the time to get to know someone before
you commit to them or their passions. What looks good on the surface may
become ugly as you dig deeper. In most cases a year is a good time frame of relational cultivation before you make a significant commitment to someone. This is
part of the discernment process. Seek to learn how this person relates to their
spouse. Look for love and respect. Their marriage relationship is a reflection of
how they will relate to you. The same can be said for their relationship with their
children. Look for patience, encouragement, responsibility, servant leadership and
forgiveness.

Whatever character traits are evident or lacking in the family environment
will hold true in other relational situations. Their true heart, however restrained,
still bubbles under the surface of their life. Anger at home means unhealthy
aggression at work. It may even rear its deceptive head in a passive-aggressive
fashion that is subversive to all. An overly critical person at home will be caustic
at work. Therefore, one good way to test the waters is to work together on a project. Have a three-month initiative and observe the relational dynamics over a
well-defined process. This gives you the opportunity to observe faithfulness and
attitude. If there is not follow-through on agreed upon goals, this is a flag
concerning future thoroughness in work. If there is a "high maintenance" attitude, then this sideways energy will become a distraction.

Before you commit to someone, discern your mutual chemistry. Look for
their ease in relating to you and others within the organization. Do not force
people to fit into an environment that is not their "wiring." The person may be a
blast to attend a sporting event with, but that may not carry over to the working
environment. Your spouse is gifted by God to discern the hearts of people. Defer
to their judgment. Be cautious in your commitment to people.

Sometimes the challenge is not the object of your commitment but your
capacity to commit. But, there must be a balance, because we all have limitations.
You will only breed frustration if you over-commit and under-deliver. This can

Dose 8

become a stumbling block to unbelievers and believers alike. Smart people do not want to embrace a belief system that is not honest and authentic. Better to say no on the front end of a commitment than to spend the implementation phase in regret.

Seek out the commitments that leverage your gifts and talents. Invest in leaders who are making a difference. Leaders commit to leaders. Life is short. Fill your commitments with exponential growth returns. Leverage your life with fewer commitments that result in greater returns. Be slow to say yes and quick to say no. People respect those who are honest about their capacity to fulfill a commitment, and they lose respect for those who commit and fail to follow through. Understand your limitations. Trust God with your noes. Be cautious in your commitment to people and projects. Wise discernment keeps you out of trouble and experiencing God's best!

God's Part

Because God knows a person's heart, He will counsel a listening believer through a spouse, through circumstances and, most importantly, through His Spirit by the application of His Word.

My Part

_____

_____

_____

_____

_____

Wayward Wife

*"It [wisdom] will save you also from the adulteress, from the wayward wife
with her seductive words, who has left the partner of her youth and ignored
the covenant she made before God."*
Proverbs 2:16-17

A wayward wife is not to be pitied by a man. She is to be
avoided. This is what wisdom requires. The role of a male friend or peer is not to
console or counsel a woman "trapped" in her marriage. If he does, there is a good
chance he will fall victim to the snare of adultery. Unhealthy marriages are
attracted to healthy marriages, and not always with the best of motives. A man
who is not wise and discerning about this risks tearing down what God has built
all these years. Certainly there is help for the wayward wife, but do not deceive
yourself into thinking that you are the one to help her out of this tormented
state.

Waywardness is a deviation from what's right. A wayward wife has strayed
from her promise of faithfulness—both to her husband and, most importantly, to
God. She has sacrificed her greatest asset, her honesty. She no longer can be trusted. She has lost her moral moorings, becoming like a boat without a rudder.
Whatever is the latest urge or impulse, she is driven by its allure. The consequences of her misguided actions mount into a reckless string of relational
tragedies. Her head is not clear and her emotions beg for attention.

This state of living did not happen overnight. A series of unwise decisions
brought her to this place—decisions not based on the truth, which lead her to
deception. One deception is thinking that she can leave a good man for a better
and more exciting life. The truth cries out, "Why leave a man who loves you
deeply with whom you have invested years of your life? You will not find anyone
more committed, loyal and loving. It is foolish to walk away from someone who
has a track record of faithfulness to you during the good times and the bad. Why
take the risk?"

Wayward wife, you need to learn to romance your husband again. Pursue
him—not some fantasy of a husband that is based on a fictional character in a
romance novel. There is no such person that has all the attributes of Jesus, a
movie star and your dad! That man does not exist nor will he ever exist. God has
given you just the husband you need. You married him because of God's leading.
God wooed him to you. It was a divine appointment. It was a God thing. He

Dose 9

sealed the deal. How can you walk away from a God-arranged marriage? It does not make sense. It is foolish. The husband of your youth loves you and your children more than life itself. There is nothing he would not do for you as long as it did not violate God's command. Cut him some slack. Look beyond his surface weaknesses to the strength of his character. He is truly a man who loves God more than he loves you, and this is a good thing. It is healthy for your marriage.

Do not drift into marital waywardness because of the wall you face. A change in circumstances will not solve these lurking issues. An ill-conceived transition will only compound them. The solution is to run toward God and your husband, not away from them. Escapism may provide short-term relief, but it will compound the problem over time. To stray is unwise and to remain wayward is foolish. Come back home to God and your husband before it is too late. They are patiently waiting for you. They love you.

Husband, love your wayward wife. Love her back to you and to God. It can be done through the power of prayer and the freedom of forgiveness. It may take God's "tough love" to shake her into her senses, but trust God to change her. Be patient!

God's Part

God orders circumstances to present a person with choices, and He provides the wisdom necessary to make the right choice.

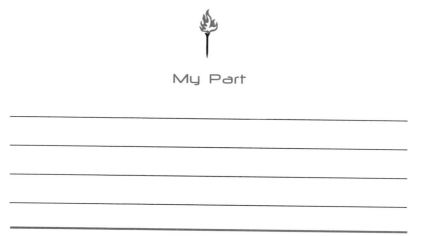

My Part

_____

_____

_____

_____

_____

Forgiveness Initiates

*"But Esau ran to meet Jacob and embraced him; he threw his arms around
his neck and kissed him. And they wept."*
Genesis 33:4

Forgiveness does not sit still. It initiates. Forgiveness is not a
frozen intellectual assent, rather it is action oriented. Forgiveness expresses itself
with love and compassion. Forgiveness that lacks initiation is not true forgiveness.
It is fake forgiveness. Forgiveness held back by the inertia of a begrudging spirit
only gives lip service. Authentic forgiveness reaches out in a way that is unnatu-
ral. The values of this world would not expect you to initiate contact with one
who hurt you deeply, but God does. The heart of forgiveness is giving something
to someone that is undeserved. The natural man and the carnal man resist this,
but the spiritual man embraces this.

Peace will come as you embrace forgiveness. Peace will invade and reign in
your heart and the heart of your offender. Reconciliation will begin as you initiate forgiveness. Just the fact that you want to get together and discuss differences
is an "olive branch." It is a way to diffuse difficult misunderstandings that evolved
into resentment. As long as a form of forgiveness crouches in the corner of self-
pity, licking its wounds, real forgiveness will lie dormant. Authentic forgiveness
moves from the head to the heart to behavior. It is like our conversion to Christ.
It may not come automatically, but over time the realities of what it means to be
born again brings us to a point of receiving the grace and forgiveness of God.

The test of spiritual maturity is your ability, by God's grace, to forgive
another. It is not always easy, but it is necessary to go deep with Christ. Stunted
growth in a relationship many times can be traced back to unforgiveness. Your
most meaningful relationships have traveled down the road of forgiveness.

So where do you start? A great place to start is prayer. Pray for the person
with whom you need to initiate forgiveness. Pray for them daily and pray for
them with compassion. Pray that they will go deep with God and learn of Him.
Pray that they will be open to your acts of forgiveness. Pray for yourself to receive
God's love and forgiveness. Pray that you will extend what you have received
from the Lord to others.

Do not be stingy with the forgiveness of Christ. Forgiveness flourishes when
it is given away. It is not meant to stay locked up in some surreal memory of the

Dose 10

past. Authentic forgiveness is fresh, relevant and alive for today. Pick up the phone and initiate a call to the one who has wounded you. Buy a plane ticket and travel to the assisted living home of your parent and spend time rekindling love and forgiving them. Drive across town and buy an ex-friend a cup of coffee or lunch. Listen intently to their fears and regrets. Extend to them forgiveness so that they can be freed to go about serving in God's Kingdom unshackled and unencumbered. Write a loving letter or an edifying e-mail to your offender. Extend the spirit of Jesus to them in words they can ponder over and over again.

God is bigger than any hurt or bitterness. His business is forgiveness. And we are in His business. Forgiveness initiates. Relationships explode with possibilities in an environment of forgiveness. Look into His face of forgiveness as Jesus hung on the cross. Let the face of Jesus be the reflection you see upon your soul. Then initiate His spirit of forgiveness to others. The cross is God's initiation toward you. In Christ, all is forgiven!

God's Part

God is the ultimate initiator of forgiveness: While we were yet sinners, Christ died for us.

My Part

_____

_____

_____

_____

_____

Seek and Save

"For the Son of Man came to seek and to save what was lost."
Luke 19:10

The lost are a target of Christ's heat-seeking love. He is passionate over their need for Himself. He initiates His grace and love while waiting patiently for a response from the lost sinner. But, unfortunately, some do not embrace His unconditional love. Indeed, some are lost and don't even know they are lost. It's scary to be lost and not realize it. This is where some pitiful souls reside. They are lost and clueless about their dire condition. Lost is a state of isolation from God and fellowship with His people. Some are lost in themselves, unable to see beyond their own selfish desires. Others are lost in their work, always busy with the next project, deadline and feverish activity. Moms become lost in their children, and husbands can become lost in their hobbies. Men can get caught up and lose their way while making money. Women can do the same while spending money.

Indeed, to be lost means that you have an opportunity to be found. This is the heart of Jesus. He pursues you at your point of seclusion and separation from Him. He wants you to be found. Once you encounter Christ, you understand that you are found out. There's no need to hide your embarrassments any longer because He already knows. He understands your humiliation and wants to replace it with humility. Since you have been exposed, now is the right time to capitulate to His love. Once He has found you, He wants to save you.

The salvation of Jesus is the greatest gift of all. He saves you from your sins to a life of growing in Him. He saves you from yourself for Himself. He saves you from an eternal hell to an eternity in heaven. He saves you from sin's control to His control. He saves you from Satan's deceptions to His realities. He saves you from lie's frustration to truth's freedom. He saves you from money's bondage to generous giving. He saves you from a mediocre life to one of abundance. He saves you from a marital battle to marital bliss. He saves you from a dysfunctional family to one that is healthy and whole. His salvation is all encompassing.

Once you are saved, you are saved thoroughly and permanently. Nothing in your life is beyond Christ's salvation. Unbelief is the only obstacle between being lost and being saved. Therefore, He is seeking moment by moment for those who will say yes to His forgiveness and grace. His soul-seeking passion is a model for

Dose II

all of us who claim the name of Christ. We have the wonderful privilege of seeking out the lost on the behalf of our Lord and Savior, Jesus. We would still be lost without the eye-opening salvation of Christ. Even while we were dead in our sins, He made us alive through faith in Christ. Gratitude for our own salvation propels us to seek out the lost.

We cannot save, but we can seek. Simple awareness of those around you in everyday life is a great start. Begin by praying for the lost. Pray for the scales of their unbelief to fall from their spiritual eyes. Pray passionately for the lost. Weep for lost souls. Pray that they will say "Yes!" to Christ. Never give up seeking the lost on behalf of Jesus Christ. Your part is to seek. His part is to save. Seek them through service. Seek them in love. Seek them in communication. Eventually "life will happen," and the sought ones will seek. The lost are more than willing candidates for salvation when the bottom falls out. This is why Jesus came to earth. This is one reason why He left the Holy Spirit on earth: He came to seek and to save the lost!

God's Part

God has shown His unconditional love for sinners through the person of His Son, the Lord Jesus Christ, who has opened the way to God and made available complete forgiveness through His atoning life, death, and resurrection.

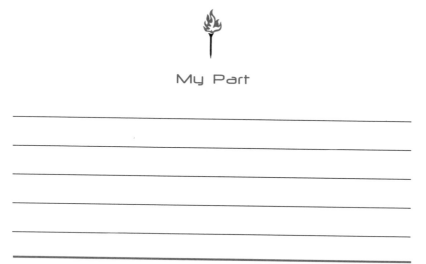

My Part

_____

_____

_____

_____

_____

Prayerful Planning

"May he give you the desire of your heart and make all your plans succeed."
Psalm 20:4

Planning is a prerequisite for anyone who desires to get results. But, prayerful planning is essential to experience God's best. After all, His best is the goal for the follower of Jesus Christ. Otherwise, we are limited to what only our efforts can produce. This self-imposed limitation is misery compared to partnering with the Almighty. We can work hard to plan—and sincerely produce a best-laid plan—but make the mistake of asking God to bless the plan after the fact. This presumes on God. He is not thrilled with the presumption of His blessing. Presumption communicates distrust and disrespect. He may choose to bless the unprayed plan, but why take the chance? And why take the credit? He will share His glory with no one.

So, a prayerless plan will leave you in a perilous position. This is an easy step to forget or to assume. You are so excited about the possibilities before you that you rush ahead without checking in with the originator of the plan. He already has the blueprints sketched out. He is a generous giver, waiting to validate your plan and even disclose part of His plan you have yet to discover. It is a beautiful process of discovery and learning. In the nighttime, as your head ponders on your pillow, He will speak to you. Through other people and circumstances, He will speak to you. Your wife or financial constraints will be accurate indicators. And obviously His Word is a great check-and-balance for your planning process. Prayerful planning keeps you married to Christ and not to the plan. Your plans will change, but He will not. What reassurance and peace our unchanging God gives.

So involve Him in the beginning and throughout the process, not just with the final draft. Like a good earthly father your heavenly Father will be engaging and helpful. He will affirm you and challenge your thinking. He will give you a perspective that may be out of the box and a little scary. God's plans are not always safe and secure from our vantage point. Sometimes His plans are risky and riling. If you are not planning prayerfully, you may miss His unconventional thinking. His way of doing something may be the very opposite of what you were originally thinking.

Dose 12

Do not be afraid of conflicting opinions. God will use this to sharpen your thinking. It is much better to have a scrubbed over plan than one that is soiled with wrong assumptions and fat with lazy thinking. Engage others to pray with you through the planning process. Especially involve those who have been where you are trying to go. Their prayers are informed and productive. They will pray from an understanding and empathetic heart. These praying saints will not throw toward heaven some half-hearted, wimpy softball. Rather, their passionate prayer will storm the throne of grace on your behalf with boldness and conviction.

Look for those whose only agenda is God's best for your life and invite them in the process of prayerful planning. Prayerful planning may slow down the process or accelerate it. Either way, it will require trust in the master planner. His overall plan is what is best. Trust Him with the results. Prayerful planning produces powerful performance!

God's Part

Our heavenly Father is the ultimate planner, and His desire is to lead and guide you in His perfect way.

My Part

_____

_____

_____

_____

_____

Calm Assurance

"'It's all right,' he said, 'Don't be afraid. Your God, the God of your father,
has given you treasure in your sacks; I received your silver.'
Then he brought Simeon out to them."
Genesis 43:23

Christ creates calm assurance. He is a shelter when disappointment rains down in sheets of insecurity. He is a rock in a stream of raging uncertainty. He is light in deepest darkness. He is a voice of reason when all hell breaks loose. The presence of the Holy Spirit in your life is your true north. Do not capitulate to the cares of this world. Stay in touch with your Savior. He is your calm assurance. Things may still get worse before they get better, but He is not going anywhere. He is there for you. Rest in Him, trust in Him and walk with Him. Listen to His still, small voice and receive His calm assurance, "It's all right." It is all right because He is all right: Jesus is just all right. He is right here with you and for you.

He also sends His emissaries of encouragement. People who seem to pop into your life become God's lifeline to heaven. They are angels of light and love. Receive those whom God has sent to you. They are God's representatives who simply by their presence say, "It's all right." Calm assurance is what these friends have to offer. They are extensions of God's grace. Place your fears at their feet and at the feet of Jesus. Let them "love on" you. You love and encourage most effectively when you allow yourself to be loved and encouraged.

We all need calm assurance. There are times fear fractures your faith. You need the tender mending of another's calm assurance to make your faith whole. The words "It's all right" are medicine for your wound. Calm assurance brings healing to your unhealthy worry. This sick situation is under God's control. He can and will handle it. He has sent this unsuspecting person into your life for calm assurance. Receive them and trust that God is orchestrating the circumstances of your life.

The transformation of your worry into calm assurance allows you to extend the same to another. Calm assurance is not the end. It is the beginning. Your newfound peace is transferable. Calm assurance is not meant to stay locked up in your stable of security. Its purpose is to be unleashed into the lives of others. Now that you are resting in the calm assurance of Christ, you can infect others

Dose 13

with the same peace and serenity. You can courier Christ to others. He has positioned you to dispatch calm assurance. The circle of your influence needs to hear you say, "It's all right."

This is leadership. Your spouse needs to hear you say, "It's all right." Your children need to hear you say, "It's all right." Your parents need to hear you say, "It's all right." Your friends need to hear you say, "It's all right." Your work associates need to hear you say, "It's all right." You need to hear you say, "It is all right!"

This is not a naïve acknowledgement. It is not the power of positive thinking or a humanistic mantra. "It's all right" is good theology. It is placing your trust in Jesus. It is a calm assurance based on the control and influence of Christ. You can be calm and assured because Christ is calm and assured. Calm assurance is a give and take. So, receive it and give it. Fear melts under the calm assurance of Christ!

God's Part

God is the author and finisher of our faith. He is in control from beginning to end. His strength and wisdom rule the universe—and our circumstances.

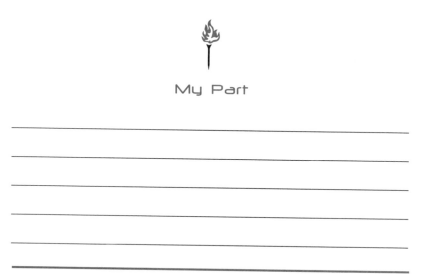

My Part

_____

_____

_____

_____

_____

Second Chance

*"…Has no one condemned you?' 'No one sir,' she said. 'Then neither do I
condemn you,' Jesus declared. 'Go now and leave your life of sin.'"*
John 8:10b-11

God is into second chances. You may not feel like you deserve a
second chance. And from a limited human perspective, you may not deserve a
second chance. This is the residue of sin. Sin, after it runs its course, leaves you in
a distasteful position. You feel beat up and used. You are embarrassed and
ashamed. The only recourse seems to be wallowing in the guilt of your shame
while receiving verbal pelts from the "righteous." This is not where God wants
you to remain.

Yes, sin brings guilt. Yes, there are those who will rub it in your face. They
may need this to cover up and soothe their own hypocrisy. Yes, sin has its consequences that you may have to live with in this life and the next. Yet in Christ you
are not condemned. You are not condemned! Christ was condemned on the cross
for the crimes of mankind. He is your passageway to freedom from sin's condemnation.

This is the beauty of laying your life prostrate before Jesus. He does not
stone you with rocks of self-righteousness. Instead, Jesus lifts up the broken
sinner and puts him back together. All the king's horses and all the king's men
cannot put you back together again, but Jesus can! He lifts you out of your
unrighteousness into His righteousness. This is the counterintuitive way of
Christ. Grace gives you a second chance.

We will all "mess up." There is no doubt about this. But, Lord willing, we
will learn from our failures and not continue in sin. To confess and repent of sin
is freedom from condemnation. To be caught in sin and then continue in sin is
condemnation. It is foolish. A fool gambles with the patience of God. When
confronted by God, capitulate. This is wisdom. Let Him lift you up, and then go
and sin no more. Therefore, there is no more condemnation in Christ.

There is a little bit of Pharisee in all of us—the condescending attitude that
elevates people over the ones they are condemning. This is the nature of pride. It
is twisted in its motivation. Somehow my public criticism of your sin tries to
justify my private sin. But, what is done in the darkness will come to light. It just
takes time, and time is infinite to God.

"He who walks with the wise grows wise, but a companion of fools suffers harm." Proverbs 13:20

Dose 14

As the accuser, be quick to confess your own sin before you judge the sin of others. This is a prerequisite. It is a big enough job to keep a clean account of one's own sins, much less try to manage the sin accounts of others. Most likely you do not have the time or expertise to be another's outsourcing for sin management. Your example of confessing and repenting of your own sin will facilitate the same in others. By God's grace you can provide a safe environment for others to work through and exit their sin. Transparency leads to healing. Give others permission to be real.

Concealed sin kills; revealed sin can lead to healing. Unconfessed sin will eat away at your body, soul and spirit. This is why we need each other. Refrain from kicking those who are down. You may be down one day and need to be lifted up. Hold back from hitting the hurting over the head with the Bible. You will hurt one day and need acceptance for healing. Give others a second chance—God has. He has for you and He has for them. Second chances are God's way. Follow the way of God. Everybody wins!

God's Part

God's grace through Christ gives people what they don't deserve—a second chance.

My Part

_____

_____

_____

_____

_____

_____

Profitable Patience

"Wait for the Lord; be strong and take heart and wait for the Lord."
Psalm 27:14

Life is normally lived waiting. We wait in lines. A teenager waits for his next birthday. We wait for job promotions. We wait for news from the doctor. We wait for the next meal. We wait for our future spouse. We wait for a lawsuit to settle. We wait for a meeting to conclude. We wait for those who have yet to keep their commitment. Every time we turn around we have an opportunity to wait.

Why wait? Most of the time we should wait because that's what is best for all parties involved. A vegetable gardener is a prisoner to waiting. However, this is seen as an asset not a liability. A tomato is much taster when it is red, large and juicy rather than green, small and hard. The smart gardener will wait for the vegetables to ripen, though He will nurture the soil along the way and keep out the weeds. There is a waiting cycle that must be completed before there is worthwhile fruit. Even when your waiting is a result of another's incompetence, you have an opportunity to grow. This holding pattern can facilitate your creativity and resourcefulness. If you did not have to wait, you may have been satisfied with how things have always been done. Now you have the opportunity to think differently.

Could there be other people or resources that can contribute to your project or plan? Because of your current inconvenience you may meet a new friend who has much more to offer than the status quo. Their experience and ideas may be the missing link you have waited for all this time. So, when things do not go as planned, see it as an opportunity to improve the plan. Indeed, the very thing may be to provide help to another instead of being consumed with your own deal. Waiting is a lesson in loving others in spite of themselves, and it even provides valued assistance during this parenthesis in your own life. Most important, however, is learning how to wait for the Lord.

What a valuable asset we have to wait upon. The Lord God Almighty is worth waiting for. It is worth waiting for His joy, because it comes to uplift us when we are sad in heart. His joy brings a smile to our face. It is worth waiting for His peace that calms our soul when we are worried in mind. His peace allows us to sleep at night. It is worth waiting for His wisdom that provides discernment

---

"He who walks with the wise grows wise, but a companion of fools suffers harm." Proverbs 13:20

Dose 15

in our conflicting options. His wisdom sets our feet on the right path. It is worth waiting for His strength that propels us through our adversity. His strength gives us confidence and perseverance for life's journey. It is worth waiting for His hope that uplifts us from our despair and depression. His hope keeps the focus on our eternal reward in heaven. He is worth the wait.

People camp out to wait and see a rock star or pay big bucks to wait and meet the president. So, waiting on God should be a cinch. Waiting is fundamentally patience with God. He is running the show. He knows what is going on. He knows what is best for you. He knows. He knows. He knows. You can trust Him in your waiting. Use this sabbatical-like time to get to know your heavenly Father more intimately. Use this time to love your family and others more than any other time in your life. Allow Him to mold your character in a way that will cause others to comment to themselves that you are different. You are different because you have been with Jesus. Waiting is not just a passage to God's blessing. It is God's blessing. Wait for the Lord. He is worth the wait!

God's Part

The Lord is not bound by time or schedules; His activities are always perfectly synchronized with His divine plan and purpose. Fellowship with Him during the wait is really the true blessing.

My Part

_____

_____

_____

_____

_____

_____

Wise Listener

"Listen now to me and I will give you some advice, and may God be with you.... Moses listened to his father-in-law and did everything he said."
Exodus 18:19a, 24

God sends people your way who offer great advice. Therefore, listen intently because you never know who may be speaking on behalf of God. These may be people you trust or distrust. Either way, do not allow pride to stand in your way of listening to what they say. Wisdom can come from the most unlikely sources; therefore, listen with discernment. Do not be a nonthinking listener. Wise listening involves a functioning brain.

The intent of wise listening is to separate the "wheat from the chaff." For example, you may be laboring away unnecessarily in stress and anxiety. Your stress may be self-inflicted. You may need a better system for processing the needs of people. You may also be trapped in the never-ending cycle of busyness. Your life and organization are more complex than even six months ago. You need a better process for handling issues and complaints. People are starting to grumble. You are weary and they are frustrated.

The most obvious adjustment may be involving others to help you serve the people or the enterprise more effectively. Take the time to recruit and train others. This takes time and trust, but if you do not start today preparing for tomorrow, you will wear out or even burn out. If this "choking point" is not remedied, you could lose your credibility. People will choose to go somewhere else, and you will lose your influence. Do not try to talk your way out of your responsibilities; rather, listen to those who are offering you advice and prayerfully consider their counsel. This may be the optimum time for you to let go and trust others. Your long-term security is not based on what you control but on what you can give away.

So who in your life is currently offering you advice and counsel? Is it your wife? Is it your father or father-in-law? Is it your mother or mother-in-law? Is it your boss? Is it your employee? Is it your friend? Are you truly listening, or are you just going through the motions and not really adjusting or modifying your behavior? There is a very good chance that the methods you have employed up to now will not propel you into the future. This time of uncertainty may be a good time to evaluate the basics of life and work. What is the purpose? What do you

"He who walks with the wise grows wise, but a companion of fools suffers harm." Proverbs 13:20

Dose 16

do best? What is your capacity? Do you value quality over quantity? Do relationships have priority over tasks? What is your motive? This honest self-evaluation, coupled with the counsel of others, will help take you to the next level of living. Moreover, listen to God. He offers clear guidance in the Holy Bible, and many, many times He is speaking directly to you through the advice of people. Do not be afraid to ask someone, "What do you think?" Pray about it and then value them and the Lord by acting on the counsel that you believe is a word from God.

If you do not take the time for wise listening, your life will translate into foolish living. A wise listener listens with a propensity for change. Without change for the better, we become worse. Listen, for He is speaking. This is wise and healthy living. Wise counsel continues for the wise listener, but it ceases for the one who chooses not to listen. We learn when we listen. God is "all about" advice and "all over" a wise listener!

God's Part

God promises to give wisdom to those who ask, and very often His delivery mechanism is an unlikely person He has put into our path.

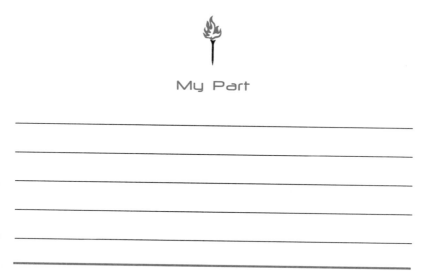

My Part

_____

_____

_____

_____

_____

_____

Trusting Obedience

*"He replied, 'The man they call Jesus made some mud and put it on my eyes.
He told me to go to Siloam and wash. So I went and washed,
and then I could see.'"*
John 9:11

Some situations call for trusting obedience. You know
what God is saying, but you are not sure of the "why" or the "how" behind His
command. What He is asking you to do may be unprecedented. This may be
your first time to follow Him in this fashion and, therefore, it is a little scary.
Some people have given you a hard time, and others think you are somewhat
strange; but this is the nature of trusting obedience. You have limited understanding but you still trust God. Though you are unsure how He is going to
provide, you trust that He will. And many times, "lo and behold," His provision
is more creative and thorough than you anticipated.

This is the fruit of trusting obedience. This is why God blesses trusting
obedience. He knows your situation. He knows your heart. He knows your
needs. He is the master at connecting your need with His provision. He uses
unconventional means so that He is guaranteed to get the glory. Yes, you could
make things happen. You could go into debt. You could manipulate a circum-
stance. You could strong-arm a relationship. You could give up or not go there,
but your impatience may rob you of God's blessing. Be obedient and trust Him
with what you know to do today. Do not be overwhelmed with tomorrow.

Trust Him with today. Be obedient today and trust Him with tomorrow. It
is trusting obedience that opens our eyes to opportunities we never imagined.
Satisfaction with conventional thinking may seem safer, but God's will is never
too risky. Following hard after God with trusting obedience is what keeps your
faith fresh and on fire. Settling into a selective obedience produces a frigid faith
that facilitates a boring, barren life with very little fruit that remains.

If God is telling you to leave, then leave. If God is telling you to stay, then
stay. If God is telling you to give, then give. If God is telling you to serve, then
serve. It is your trusting obedience that He blesses in spades. Fuel all your efforts
by faith. This will stretch you and grow you. God may not show up until the last
minute. Others may criticize your God-sized mission and your faith-filled methods. Because of fear of your failure, friends may disassociate or distance themselves from you, but once they see God's blessing and faithfulness, they will come

Dose 17

out of hiding and attempt to ride the bandwagon. Therefore, do not let the fickleness of people's support dissuade you from trusting obedience. God is the one to whom you will ultimately give an account. As long as you can explain to God your actions, you are in a good position.

If you disobey God, prepare for a severe judgment. Followers of Jesus have tasted the fruit of trusting obedience. There is no reason to return to the wilderness of distrustful disobedience. Your trusting obedience may relate to money. Hold finances with an open hand and watch God work. Money can be God's tool to facilitate His work, or it can be Satan's obstacle that keeps you from trusting obedience. Listen intently to the voice of Jesus, and then trust Him and do what He says. He has your best interest in mind. His intent is not harm but healing. Your trusting obedience will fuel the faith of others and bring glory to God. You are not alone. He is with you. You can trust Him with your obedience. Do what He says. Clarity and understanding follows trusting obedience. Trust and obey—this is His best way!

God's Part

God's ways may not be completely understood, but faithful obedience to His call always brings blessing.

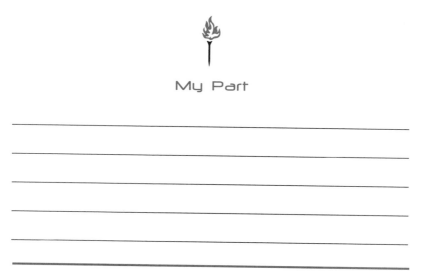

My Part

_____

_____

_____

_____

_____

Poor Judgment

"But a man who commits adultery lacks judgment;
whoever does so destroys himself."
Proverbs 6:32

Poor judgment is the result of a series of unwise decisions. Poor judgment does not develop overnight—it is the fruit of decisions void of wisdom. Because the outcomes are time delayed, you may not see the immediate effects of poor judgment. But, eventually the harvest from unwise decisions will come: folly at best and destruction at worst.

Discipline is designed by God to be a friend of wise decision-making. It is the man who becomes undisciplined in his thought life who wanders down the road of poor judgment. Avoid that road at all costs. Bandits are lurking there ready to pounce on you. The bandit of lust will steal your time by preoccupying you with books, magazines and Web sites that feed your sex-crazed mind.

Lust left unbridled will run rampant until your sexual appetite grows addictive. You will soon lose the joy found in the bride of your youth. You will think you need something more exciting, something more tantalizing. This is a lie straight from the enemy's playbook. A self-centered, lust-driven man can never be satisfied. You are playing with fire and will inevitably be burned.

One of God's remedies for temptation is the exercise of discipline. As a follower of Jesus Christ you are to take every thought captive to Him. This is not a game of cat-and-mouse. This is a matter of life and death. Disease is another bandit waiting to steal from you as you meander down this road of poor judgment. You take a humongous health risk when you engage in sex outside of the bounds of marriage. You imperil your physical, emotional and spiritual health. This is poor judgment. Indeed, this destructive lifestyle borders on the insane. Sin will lead you to do strange things and this one is all too common.

Wise judgment on the other hand is the fruit of discipline and boundaries. You are wise to develop disciplines over time that feed your love for your wife. Time with God is certainly foundational as you regularly feed your mind with the truth of Scripture. Your wife is God's gift to be cherished and honored. A happy wife is a happy life. Romance her and woo her with your time, money and respect. How you treat your wife contributes greatly to who she becomes. If you value her, she feels great worth and significance. This value statement can come

Dose 18

in the form of listening to her opinions and applying them to your home and relationships. You respect her when you do not force your decisions on her, but rather pray and wait on her to sense the same direction and purpose. You lovingly lead instead of being a demanding dictator. Communicate with her often through written notes, e-mails and phone calls. Laugh and cry together, pray together. Take her shopping, especially shopping for shoes.

These are disciplines that give couples a scary advantage over the average lost soul responding to any woman that gives him the least bit of attention. The best remedy for adultery is a vibrant, growing and on-fire marriage that has Christ as the centerpiece. Unravel your emotions from around the axle of lust and love your wife passionately and with abandonment. Be alone with no other woman but her. This is wise judgment. Start wise living today!

God's Part

God is faithful to place roadblocks in your way should you stumble down the perilous road to adultery. He pricks your conscience; He gives you friends for accountability.

My Part

_____

_____

_____

_____

_____

Stand Alone

*"Do not follow the crowd in doing wrong. When you give testimony in a
lawsuit, do not pervert justice by siding with the crowd."*
Exodus 23:2

To stand alone means that you take a stand for what is
right. There should be no confusion between right and wrong; however, debate
about it is ongoing. This is why it is critical to get your moral definitions from
God's Word. Some things like dishonesty, murder, idolatry, adultery, drunken-
ness, cheating, stealing, pride, unforgiveness and laziness are clearly defined moral
issues that need not be compromised. Individuals, families, organizations and
governments who tolerate immorality will become its victim.

At the same time, society may be insistent on rewriting the rules of decent
behavior. You and your influence may be one of the few resistors to the majority's
malaise. Do not give in to the pressure to compromise your convictions. You
know the financial ruin that seduces those sucked into gambling's grip. The lie of
gambling is that nobody gets hurt; it is mere entertainment. The truth is that it
strips dignity and decency from a person and everyone associated with them.
Stand alone in this battle over money.

You know that human life begins in the womb. The lie of abortion is that
freedom to choose overrides the protection of life. The truth is that abortion kills
babies and it kills the parents' respect for themselves. Stand alone in this battle
over life. You know that marriage is meant for a man and a woman. The lie of
homosexuality is that people have a right to enjoy same-sex relations. The truth is
that homosexuality is relational perversion. Stand alone in this battle over
marriage. The whims of the crowd come and go. Your God-given convictions are
meant to remain. Stand alone at work, in school and in your community.

When you stand alone, you still have God. So to stand alone does not mean
you are isolated from Him. On the contrary, when you choose to make a stand
for what's right, your walk with God goes to a whole other level. While the
crowd subscribes to what is wrong, He smiles when He sees you stand up for
right. There is a warning, however: Do not become proud of being right. God is
the one who has given you clarity of conviction and keenness of vision. If
anything, your attitude will become more humble and trusting in Him. The spirit of Jesus is your greatest defense. Use His methods of teaching truth, reaching

Dose 19

out to the sinners and rebuking the religious hypocrites. Jesus was firm, fair and friendly. We can be and do no less as we stand alone against the onslaught of unrighteousness. Indeed, to stand alone is to stand with God and to stand with His godly followers.

Do not fall into the temptation of turning on each other. We are all in the process of becoming more like Christ. If we can agree on these large issues, then smaller ones will eventually take care of themselves. So, fear God and abhor sin. Love people and take a stand for what is right. There is a good chance the crowd will carry you over the cliff of godly convictions. Instead, you become the influencer. The crowd is your mission field. Serve it with humility, grace and persistence. Sometimes members of the crowd will awaken and come over to your side. Keep shining the light of your life and the light of truth into their eyes. You never know who might respond. Stand alone for the sake of your faith, of your family, for God's sake and for the crowd. What you do and say matters. Steward it wisely. Choose Christ over the crowd!

God's Part

God promises to stand by the one who stands alone for Him.

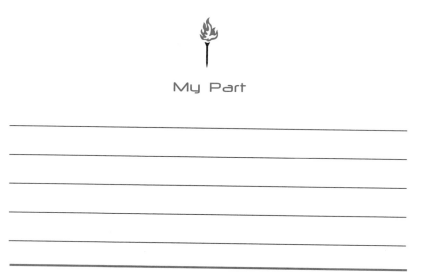

My Part

_____

_____

_____

_____

_____

No Comparison

"When Peter saw him, he asked, 'Lord what about him?'"
John 21:21

Do not fall into the comparison trap. It is easy to do. As children, this happens all the time through sibling rivalries. Your common concern became how your brother or sister's treatment compared with how you were treated. Inevitably someone cried foul. The complaint went something like, "That's not fair!" This is what comparison does. It breeds discontent and a sense of unfairness. This comparison game gets you into trouble every time. It is not healthy.

Comparisons may start with childlike conniptions, progress to teen tantrums, and then settle into adult animosity. If you are the person comparing, you lose. You never feel like you quite measure up, or you feed your pride with your sense of superiority. The comparison game includes your looks: Your wrinkles, your hair (or lack of hair), your weight and private body parts all seem inadequate to the outside world of "perfection." This is an unrealistic and unfair game to play. You will always lose. There will always be someone with a sleeker and more wrinkle-free body. The same can be said for possessions. If you compare your house and car to others, you will live in perpetual disappointment. There is a continual flow of families who have the next bigger and better home and automobile. If acquisition of stuff is your goal, you will never have enough, and there will be someone else who has a little bit more.

The comparison trap can even be set in your spiritual life. If you could just have as much faith as the other "godly" person you know. If you could just pray like they pray, give like they give and serve like they serve. Or, you complain to God because sinners seem to get off scot-free, while you are penalized for what seems to be a much lesser offense. The comparison game is a vicious circle that never stops. Get off this merry-go-round of discontent. Instead, embrace and celebrate the accomplishments of others. Let others inspire you to greater heights, not drive you with an unhealthy desire to compare.

God is the plumb line. He is your reference for reality. Let Christ be your point of comparison. You seek Him first and His plan for you. Your plan is unique to your personality, giftedness, experiences and place in life. Stay the course in becoming more like Jesus. Aspire to His example and comply in obedi-

Dose 20

ence to His direction, commands, principles and values for your life. Each day is a recalibration and alignment with His will. Fulfill your special place in the Body of Christ. A productive comparison is reviewing where you are today compared to where God has brought you. His faithfulness is real and undeniable. He is the undisputed champion of keeping His Word and taking care of His own. Compare Him to any other god of this world, and nothing is even a close second. God blows away any category of comparison. No one's love, holiness and grace can rival His.

He is the author of them all. Love—God is the unconditional lover of men and women. Holiness—God's wrath is to be feared above anything or anyone else. Grace—God's grace is unmerited, undeserved and available to all. Therefore, resist comparing to others. Stay content in Christ. Be inspired and motivated by aligning your expectations with God's will for your life. And, lastly, be encouraged by understanding that nothing in this life holds a candle compared to the matchless and incorruptible character of God. Compare God and not people. There is no comparison with either!

God's Part

God's plan for each individual is custom-fit and as unique as the snowflakes.

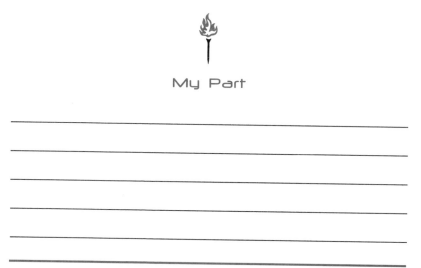

My Part

_____

_____

_____

_____

_____

Authentic Living

*"Blessed is the man whose sin the Lord does not count against him
and in whose spirit is no deceit."*
Psalm 32:2

Authentic living is real living. You are a bona fide believer in Christ. You are a genuine follower of Jesus Christ. Your faith commitment is unquestioned. You are the real deal. In your life what you see is what you get. Pretense and guile are a distant memory for you. There is nothing counterfeit about your character. This is authenticity. Authenticity does not mean you are without sin. On the contrary, authenticity means you confess your sin to God and others. People don't feel intimidated by your holiness. Rather, they feel encouraged by your transparency. You are a fellow struggler, daily dependent on God's grace.

Death to self is a moment-by-moment choice in your life. You have not arrived. You are just getting started. The more you mature in your faith, the more you feel the need for maturity in your faith. People may look to you as a good example, but this humbles you and scares you. You are not proud of any good thing in your life. Goodness comes from God—He deserves the credit—but you recognize God's blessing for what it is, and you are very, very grateful for His goodness. Your authentic living is like a magnet. Others are drawn to your openness and honesty. There is not a deceitful bone in your body. You recognize and admit that without God and people in your life, you would be much the lesser person.

This authentic attitude attracts not only good people but great people. Great people do not want to be around perfect people. Instead, they want to hang out with others who understand their own weaknesses and even smile about them. Authentic people know how to laugh at themselves. As they get older, they take themselves less seriously and they take God more seriously. When you admit to your blind spots, people understand better how to support you in your weakness. Instead of people thinking less of you for your admission of weakness, they believe in you even more. Authenticity feeds respect, while deceit harvests disrespect. Nonetheless, authenticity begins with God.

Because God is 100% authentic, He expects the same from His children. There is nothing at all deceitful about God. His Word is His Word, true and

Dose 21

everlasting. You can trust His promises. There is no need to try to hide from God. Your authenticity with the Almighty tells Him what He already knows. This disarmament is more for you than for God. It is a relief when you can lay down your struggles with anger, lust, gossip and greed. Concealed sin is the issue. Cover up and you are unable to come clean with God and others. He knows what you are hiding and, if the truth be known, so do others. The truth will escape from your finite grip. He is looking for those authentic followers whom He can bless even more.

Authentic believers are blessing receivers because they are truth givers. Yes, it is wise to be discreet in your transparency with others. A good start is to say here are my weaknesses, what others do you see? This authenticity will free you and free others to be the Body of Christ—supporting, encouraging and holding each other accountable. Be authentic as He is authentic and, as a result, we will all experience the real thing!

God's Part

God takes pleasure in authenticity, because it is a reflection of who He is.

My Part

_____

_____

_____

_____

_____

Unintentional Sin

"The Lord said to Moses,...'Say to the Israelites, "When anyone sins unintentionally...if the whole community sins unintentionally...when a leader sins unintentionally and does what is forbidden in any of the commands of the Lord his God, he is guilty."'"
Leviticus 4:1-2, 13a, 22a

Unintentional sin requires intentional actions. You can sincerely sin unknowingly, but this does not diminish your guilt or your sin's effect. Indeed, unintentional sins may do the most harm. They are harmful because the offender is unaware of their sinful stealth behavior. There is an inoculation to sin's presence. It is a scary place to live. You may be treating your spouse in a subtle but sinful way. It may be silence when you need to speak, or speaking when you need to be silent. Your behavior may seem totally innocuous to you, but in reality it is hideously harmful to him or her. Your acidic actions may be unintentional, but the hurtful consequences are still alive and well. Do not justify your sarcastic humor by claiming to be "just kidding." What was intended to be a joke can easily evolve into a put-down and deep discouragement. You may have intended to build up, but in reality you tore down.

Good intentions do not guarantee best results. They may even lead to bad behavior. You cannot justify unintentional sin. This is tempting. After all, you did not mean to sin. However, where you meant to encourage, you discouraged. Where you meant to help, you hurt. Where you meant to serve, you provided a disservice. Where you meant to make things easier, you made them harder. Your motive may have been pure, but the results of your unintentional sins are still real. It is time to stop this vicious cycle and become intentional in confession and repentance. Shift your energy and efforts toward asking for forgiveness and changing your behavior.

Another key element is to be intentional in understanding and obeying the Lord's commands. This process of education and application will preclude a lot of sinning unintentionally. His ways are what's best. His path is paved with the right intentions, which in turn produce right results. God's ways are the best ways. By the power of His Holy Spirit, He can lead you out of a harsh relational environment to one of humility and helpfulness. He can replace the insecurities that drive you with security that allows you to rest in Him.

Dose 22

His commands are healthy and good. Be intentional in acknowledging His calming presence and His gratuitous grace. This is the path to peace with God and peace with people. Be intentional to listen first to God before you speak to people or about people. Be intentional to extend mercy to others; there is a good chance they will do the same back to you. Be intentional to not sin unintentionally and life will become better.

Mostly, be intentional with your heavenly Father. He is there waiting for you. He is waiting to forgive. He is waiting to give wisdom. He is waiting to extend comfort. He is waiting to calm your fears. Be intentional with the Lord. and He will lead you away from unintentional sins toward people. And when you do blow it, He will be there to forgive and redirect your path. The road to sin can be paved with good intentions, but the road to God is paved with right intentions. He will lead you to be intentional in doing what's right, so that you avoid unintentionally doing what's wrong. God is "into" intentionality. Therefore, be intentional with Him!

God's Part

Every action of God is for a purpose; He never does anything unintentionally.

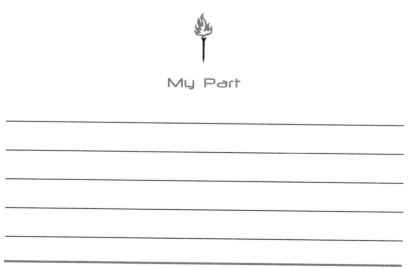

My Part

_____

_____

_____

_____

_____

Good Versus Best

"So the Twelve gathered all the disciples together and said, 'It would not be right for us to neglect the ministry of the word of God in order to wait on tables.'"
Acts 6:2

Many times good is the enemy of the best. Your competition for God's best is not necessarily gross sin or bad things. Good things are what usually distract you from your sweet spot. Do not be lured into this lesser approach to life. Everybody else's agenda for you does not equal God's agenda. Yes, the needs are great, but a need does not constitute an action, much less a call. This is where your courage of conviction can keep you from unwisely spreading yourself too thin. If you are scattered about in a multitude of activities, there is a good chance you will miss the focused opportunity of God's best.

Resist the temptation to be an inch deep and a mile wide. Rather, drill down on divinity's call on your life. You know how you are wired and gifted. Validate what you do best with others who know you well. Tap into their wisdom and discernment. Your present predicament may be the result of overcommitment and under-ability. You can always tell when you are not operating in the vortex of your giftedness. These worthy and good activities become a chore. Something haunts you. It is the realization that another talented person in this needed area could do a much better job than you with half the effort. It is sobering, but true. So have the courage to find a replacement for this good activity so you can focus on what you do best.

What you do best is admired by others. They celebrate your God-given skills. This is the role we all need to find for ourselves. Position yourself to excel in what you do best. However, that means having the courage and the faith to say no to good people and to good things. Mature people will understand. Others may give you a hard time. But, you can be at peace when you are in the crosshairs of God's best.

If you are a gifted teacher, do not be distracted by all the opportunities that scream for your service. There are others who can serve but are unable to teach. In fact, a server might even aspire to teach because they value the outcome of helping people. But, the amount of preparation and energy exerted toward this educational endeavor is not the best use of their time. There is another example

Dose 23

of experiencing God's best. It is relational investments. Right relationships many times will trump other good tasks or activities. Children are children for a season. Attending their ball games instead of another hour at the office is what's best. Parents are parents for a finite period of time. Sitting on the front porch with them and watching the grass grow is better than an occasional distant e-mail or even a phone call. Physical exercise is important, but training in godliness is better. Meeting a project deadline is strategic, but listening to a person in distress may be the greater priority.

Do not bow to the good when the best is waiting in the wings to dance. Dance with the best, and the good will take care of itself. God's role is to handle the good while you focus on the best. It is a step of faith, but He can be trusted with the good and the best. Do not settle for the crumbs of the good. Instead, feast on the best!

God's Part

God has specific assignments tailored for you to do that no one else can do quite as well.

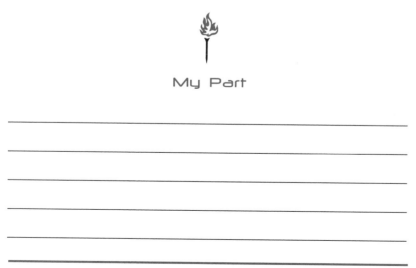

My Part

_____

_____

_____

_____

_____

Affliction's Avoidance

"...I am a dread to my friends—those who see me on the street flee from me.
I am forgotten by them as though I were dead; I have become like broken pottery."
Psalm 31:11b-12

Do not forget the afflicted, because those who are afflicted are usually avoided. The affliction could be health woes, financial challenges or a relational crisis. The truth is that people are repelled by high-maintenance individuals. After all, we need people who will provide us value, not drag us down with their misfortune. We devise various excuses to avoid the afflicted. Health-related issues are really between the person and their physician. These are private matters. This is none of my business, right? Plus, I never know what to say. Financial stress is the result of bad choices and irresponsible planning; therefore they should suffer the consequences. I do not need to bail them out, do I?

Relational issues are complicated. There are always two sides to the story, and it takes an exorbitant amount of time and effort to get all the facts. Don't I need to be a wise steward of my time? There is truth in all of these statements; however, no matter how you slice it the afflicted need acceptance. Avoidance comes easy, but acceptance takes effort. What a difference one committed friend makes in the middle of a disaster. That one "stand by your man" kind of attitude may be the very thing God uses to prevent this desperate person from giving up. Do not underestimate the value of your involvement. Several people doing something add up to a lot in the eyes of the afflicted. We can give up on those afflicted only when our heavenly Father gives up on them. This means we are in for the long haul.

God is patient and longsuffering. At one time or another we have needed or will need the longsuffering of God in our life. Up to this point your life afflictions may have been relatively light. If so be grateful, but do not let your personal detachment from affliction detach you from the afflicted.

You may lack the firsthand experience and emotional empathy, but you do not lack the example of Jesus. This cannot be dismissed. The very people Jesus went to were the lame, the blind and the lepers. In other words He loved the outcasts of society. He went out of His way to spend time with sinners. The adulteress, people living together, murderers, liars, the greedy and those with messed-

Dose 24

up motives. He sought out these self-centered misfits. He actually expressed His acceptance by spending social time in their homes. He was a friend of sinners. He was drawn to the afflicted rather than repulsed. Jesus provides the best refresher course on how to reach out to and love those suffering from affliction. He is the case study we need to research.

The hardest person to accept may be the person who does not want to change. However, God can still change their "want to." Do not write off or give up on anyone; let them make that choice. Always provide an environment of acceptance for the afflicted. Pursue them as is appropriate and default regularly to forgiveness and compassion. Accept the afflicted, for this is the way of Jesus. Accept the afflicted, because there is a good chance you will one day need acceptance in your affliction. And, by God's grace, beautiful lives will rise from the ashes of affliction.

God's Part

Jesus is our guide for how to minister to the afflicted. He perfectly knows their situation, and He perfectly knows how they feel: He personally suffered the most extreme affliction imaginable.

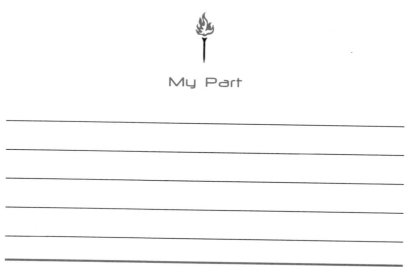

My Part

_____

_____

_____

_____

_____

Fruitful Living

"When you enter the land and plant any kind of fruit tree, regard its fruit as forbidden. For three years you are to consider it forbidden; it must not be eaten. In the fourth year all its fruit will be holy, an offering of praise to the Lord. But in the fifth year you may eat its fruit. In this way your harvest will be increased. I am the Lord your God."
Leviticus 19:23-25

Good things take time. It is through the process of maturation that fruit is produced. Fruit comes over time. The fruit of profitability takes time when you are growing a business. The fruit of trust grows over time as you develop relationships. The fruit of life change eventually takes root when a ministry is just getting started. The fruit of a family's love and loyalty take root in the fertile soil of acceptance and forgiveness. The fruit of the Spirit is a lifelong process of sanctification and growth in the human character. Financial fruit compounds with time as proper care and attention is applied to giving, saving and wise spending.

There is a process of fruitful living that God has put into place that benefits us all. But, fruitful living requires patience and trust in the Lord. It is a long-term perspective, with focused steps along the way, that builds a fruitful life and a fruitful way of thinking. If you are just a consumer of life's fruit, you are missing the fulfilling opportunity of fruitful living. Fruitful living means that you are a part of the process of preparation, care and the harvesting of fruit. Your investment in your family is an example of this fruitful process. You may not see fruit for years, or the fruit may be green, sour or bruised. Nevertheless, you remain faithful to invest in your marriage and children, realizing the fruits of your labor are not in vain. One day your child will thank you for taking time to meet his friends and getting to know his friends' parents. This is part of helping children develop a vineyard of healthy relationships. This simple process of investigation and accountability will serve them well the rest of their lives.

In the same way, God is growing a strong taproot of trust in your life. You may not see much evidence of His fruit today, but remain faithful and one day you will. This level of long-term maturation with Jesus will bear fruit beyond your wildest dreams. Be patient with God. He is working in and through you. You want the fruit to explode in outward results, but He is still doing an inward work of grace in your heart and mind. External fruit follows internal fruit. The fruit of the heart and mind produce fruit both in quality and quantity.

"He who walks with the wise grows wise, but a companion of fools suffers harm." Proverbs 13:20

Dose 25

Do not fall into the trap of comparison to others. You may not understand totally their circumstances, or God may have chosen to bless them in a unique way. We are all a work in progress. My fruit-bearing preparation and experience will probably look differently from yours. However, God can be trusted. He is in control. What you desired yesterday may not happen until tomorrow.

So, don't give up on God, or His process of fruitful living. Poor is the individual that lacks fruit. Rich are the ones who have persevered in the process and now experience spiritual fruit, relational fruit, financial fruit and physical fruit beyond measure. One who just consumes the fruit of others is in danger of ingratitude and discontentment. But, those who stay engaged in the fruit-bearing process of waiting and trusting remain joyful in Jesus. Today's patience leads to tomorrow's productivity. If you live in the past, you live in regret. If you live in the future, you live in fear. If you live in the present, you live in peace. This is fruitful living!

God's Part

God is both the fruit tender and the fruit inspector. He knows exactly what's needed to produce fruit that ultimately brings glory to Him.

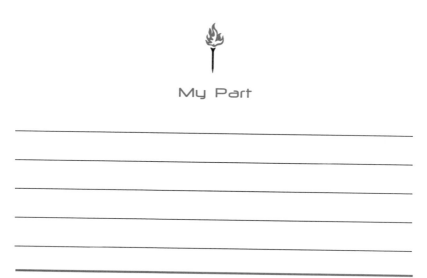

My Part

_____

_____

_____

_____

_____

Quick Change

"When they came up out of the water, the Spirit of the Lord suddenly took Philip away, and the eunuch did not see him again, but went on his way rejoicing."
Acts 8:39

Change can happen fast. It may be health change. It could be career change. It may be good or bad change involving finances. Life is about cycles of change. A relationship can be here today and gone tomorrow. It is nobody's fault, but it is part of God's process. Many times He is behind change. God is the ultimate change agent. He changes seasons. He changes hearts. He changes weather. He changes life to death. He changes death to life. He can convene change because He never changes. It is reassuring to rest in our unchanging heavenly Father. But, it can be disconcerting to experience change, especially sudden change. It is this unpredictability that rattles our cages. We like life neat and in clearly defined categories—but the reality of life is change. Categories become redefined and their locations shift.

This is where you need to remain nimble. Do not become set in your ways. Anything you hold with a tight fist is a candidate for God's removal. You cannot trust Him with everything and leave out this one thing. Trust in God is all-inclusive. Anything that you exempt from God's trust can be easily removed. Change may be a part of God's process of shaking loose anything you may be gripping too tightly. This change is an opportunity to trust. Proper perspective is critical during change. Look at change as a friend not a foe.

Remember that God's change is what is best for all parties. Those you have invested in are changed forever. Some have been changed for eternity because they have met Jesus and have received Him by faith into their lives. Others have been changed from timid believers to bold followers of Christ. Fear has changed to peace. Sadness has changed to joy. God has used you to facilitate positive change in the lives of people.

The most effective way to deal with change is to anchor your faith in your unchanging heavenly Father. He is your compass during a storm of change. He is your moral conscience as temptations assault you during change. He is your rock of hope when the fear of change floods your soul. He is your stability as you experience the instability of change, especially quick change. Do not be crushed

Dose 26

by the swelling waves of change. Instead ride them to a deeper walk with Jesus. Use change as an invitation into a closer relationship with Jesus. Look to God as the conductor who is orchestrating your current concert of change. Listen for the harmony and melody that He has beautifully composed just for you. Change is not a shrill noise to be tolerated. Change is God's pleasant ode inviting you to intimacy with the Almighty. Yes this change may seem abrupt and discombobulated. But once you process the initial shock, take it as a sign of the Spirit's work.

Sometimes we need a jolt to drive us to Jesus. You don't want to get too comfortable. Change is inevitable. Change is God's tool to mold us more into the image of His son Jesus. Follow the Holy Spirit, and you will change, people around you will change and circumstances will change. Change means that God is at work. Be concerned only if you are not changing. You can trust God explicitly during this change. However quick or calculated change has been, He is unchanging and can be trusted!

God's Part

God has designed change to be part of a believer's process of sanctification—becoming more like Jesus.

My Part

_____

_____

_____

_____

_____

_____

Opportunity's Window

*"He who gathers crops in summer is a wise son, but he who sleeps
during harvest is a disgraceful son."*
Proverbs 10:5

Some opportunities can be seasonal, which means it is
important to "make hay while the sun shines." It is also a warning to not assume
that your current opportunity will always remain, at least in its current form. Do
not take your opportunity for granted. Thank God for it every day and ask Him
how to steward its value. Certainly it involves allowing others to leverage a new
opportunity from yours. Opportunities are not to be hoarded; rather, they are to
be dispensed. Remember those who believed in you and were stepping stones to
this opportunity. If it were not for their confidence in you and your abilities, you
would still be languishing. Do not forget where you came from. Avoid pride and
egotism. This happens when you spread the love. You can become an opportunity creator because of the opportunities afforded to you by others.

The one thing greater than enjoying opportunity is giving opportunity. Pray
today for a faithful friend and invite them to join you during this window of
time. The engagement may be short and impacting or long and enduring—let
God figure out those dynamics. It is up to you to steward your current opportunity with prayer and generosity. Do not take it for granted. It may be here today
and gone tomorrow. Keep your financial house in order in preparation for opportunity's transition. Presumption on the future is not a wise choice to make. You
could risk losing everything. Consolidate your resources and protect yourself
from the worst-case scenario. Ultimately the future is in God's hands but give
Him your faithfulness, not your foolishness, to work with.

God is the opportunity maker. Thank Him often and give Him the credit
for your good fortune. Don't just tip God with recognition, but truly integrate
your faith into the workplace. He does not need patronizing, rather He desires
passionate followers who engage the culture on His behalf. It is the difference
between God as an "add on" or as "standard equipment" for our travel through
life. Pray for opportunities that will broaden your platform to be an influencer
for God.

Opportunity is for a Kingdom purpose. As you manage your current opportunity well, God can trust you with additional opportunities. Do not feel the

Dose 27

pressure to make things happen. God can deliver to you more deals than you can say grace over. He is the consummate Kingdom deal maker. Also, you may not be quite ready for the "big deal." It could be that in your present season of life you need to give attention to weightier matters like education, training, marriage foundations, children's activities, character development and spiritual maturity.

Use this perceived parenthesis in life to learn new things, such as how to be a better manager and leader. Learn how to run a meeting efficiently and effectively. Do the same with your time management and administrative skills. Get to know God, your wife and children so that when an opportunity arises, you can attack it from a position of strength. Ask God for wisdom and faith on which opportunities to take and which to let pass by. And when you are in the middle of a grand opportunity, go for it. Wear it out and then rest when it is over. You have a window of time. Use it for God's glory before it shuts!

God's Part

As the consummate deal maker, God entrusts opportunities to you and gives you wisdom and faith to manage them well.

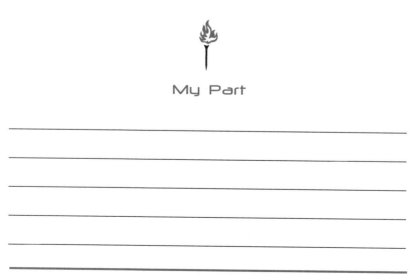

My Part

_____

_____

_____

_____

_____

Fear's Discouragement

"And they spread among the Israelites a bad report about the land they had explored. They said, 'The land we explored devours those living in it. All the people we saw are of great size.'…'Only do not rebel against the Lord. And do not be afraid of the people of the land, because we will swallow them up. Their protection is gone, but the Lord is with us. Do not be afraid of them.'"
Numbers 13:32, 14:9

Fear discourages. It discourages you from obedience to God. It discourages you from trusting God. It discourages you from enjoying God's blessing. Fear is the great discourager. Discouragement resides in the back pocket of fear. They thrive on one another. You cannot have one without the other. Your fear will lead you to discouragement, and your discouragement will lead you to fear. It is a vicious cycle of discontent. The fearful love to recruit others to their side. Somehow this justifies their fearfulness.

The fearful people in your life are normally the loudest. Their fears drive them to spread fear like wildfire. They tend to whip others into a fearful frenzy. However, before you join their bandwagon of bad reports, check out their story. Make sure the facts support their fear. Indeed, fear is one of Satan's most effective strategies. He is a promoter of fear. His goal is to preoccupy you in fear so that you do not face the realities of God's peace and protection. God is with you.

There is no need to fear. In fact, if you continue in your fears, you are rebelling against the Lord. Your chronic state of fear is closing God out of your circumstances. God cannot be boxed out. He is with you whether you acknowledge Him or not. So, rise up from your fearful state and put on your confidence in Christ. His grace is sufficient. He is working out all things for His purpose. Stay fixed on Him and your fears will subside. Be consumed with Christ and your cares will grow faint without fear. Do not feed fear. Starve it until it shrivels and dies.

God has given you this vision. It is His gift to you. It is yours for the taking. Do not be discouraged over the timing of its culmination. Your God-given vision may be dormant for now, but a dormant vision is not a dead vision. You may be experiencing a momentary pause for the sake of preparation. There are other people and resources that need cultivation and development. Your own maturity and capacity for responsibility need expansion. It is now that God is preparing you to handle the next steps of His vision for your life. Use this time of uncer-

Dose 28

tainty to grow your faith and to drown your fears. There are two choices that invite you to decide daily. One is fear and the other is faith. Faith will trump fear if you let it. Faith is the heat that melts the cold, icy grip of fear. Faith in God frees you from the inertia of fear. Fear discourages. Faith encourages. Fear flees. Faith stays. Fear gives up. Faith digs in. Fear questions. Faith trusts. Fear sees obstacles. Faith sees opportunities. Fear weakens. Faith strengthens.

Use this test of your faith to go deeper with Christ. Untested faith weakens, but tested faith strengthens. Be encouraged. Fear is overrated. Faith in Christ is underrated. He is your confidence. In the face of fear He can be trusted!

God's Part

God's message is always the same when He encounters a person of faith: "Fear not!"

My Part

_____

_____

_____

_____

_____

Disagreement's Division

"They had such a sharp disagreement that they parted company. Barnabas took Mark and sailed for Cyprus, but Paul chose Silas and left, commended by the brothers to the grace of the Lord."
Acts 15:39-40

Two good people can have two very good points.

Their points may be opposed, but both of their applications are good. This is why it is OK to disagree. In fact, disagreement may be necessary in some cases to promote God's agenda. You might not be where you are today were it not for a disagreement. Disagreements can easily propel you forward in the right direction.

Do not fear disagreements. Instead, fear what might happen if you fail to disagree. The fruit of incompetence might have continued were you not bold enough to disagree. You might stew in your frustration as it turns to rage without the outlet disagreement provides. If you don't disagree, you will become angry with yourself for not standing up for what you really think. Therefore, do not let a relational bully push you around. Stand up to his manipulative façade and face him with the facts of the situation. He may try to "bob and weave" his way out of your accurate definition of the surrounding circumstances. However, stand your ground with grace and conviction.

It is OK to disagree. If two people always agree, then one of them is unnecessary. This is the genius of marriage. Marriage is designed for disagreement. Otherwise, neither the man nor the woman would ever grow in depth of character, while rooting out bad habits. Your spouse disagrees with you because they love you. They love you enough to not allow you to remain where you are. Your spouse is your biggest fan. You lose if their concerns revert to silence because of your rejection over any disagreements. Instead, leverage your disagreements into making you both better. For example, she desires to wait on an investment because of her financial conservatism; so, a wise husband waits. He waits to honor her, and he waits by trusting God for the right timing!

There may even be times to separate from a friend over a disagreement. You have made suggestions that seem to fall on deaf ears. You are frustrated and feel that there is a better way. Both of you believe God is on your side. This is a situation where prayer is paramount. Pray for a spirit of reconciliation, not rejection. Pray that you will value the other person despite the definite disagreement. Pray

Dose 29

for an attitude of respect and understanding as you work through this process of disagreement. Indeed, it is much easier to ignore this 800-pound elephant in the room, but ignoring just delays the consequences and compounds their effect. So, seek an amicable division of relationships and resources. Be fair so that both of you can hit the ground running for God. Be honest and forthright with your needs, but bend toward the needs of your friend. God will bless your open and unselfish spirit.

This prayerful process, pregnant with godly counsel, is what God blesses. He may very well multiply the division resulting from your disagreement. It is a matter of emphasis. God will bless your emphasis on grace, and will equally do the same with your friend's emphasis on truth. Satan tries to thwart and destroy through disagreements. However, God uses disagreements to create and build His Kingdom. Disagreements can be a diving board into a deeper walk with Christ. Do not be afraid to go there. Disagreements divide us over ideologies and methods, but, over time, they draw us closer to God and each other!

God's Part

God will bless His work—despite diverse methods and diverse individuals—as long as it is truly His work.

My Part

_____

_____

_____

_____

_____

_____

Financial Faithfulness

"The wicked borrow and do not repay, but the righteous give generously."
Psalm 37:21

The use of money is an indicator of a person's heart.
Generosity or greed, maturity or immaturity, faithfulness or unfaithfulness—
these are all motives exposed by money. Every dollar has a motive attached.
Money is neutral but not its use. Borrowing money is not a sin, but not repaying
the debt labels you as wicked—harsh words but true. This is reason enough to be
faithful in our financial obligations and even more reason to avoid debt. In fact
why not avoid debt unless it is absolutely necessary? Possible exceptions might be
for a home mortgage, especially if you pay it off as soon as possible. Or, it might
be prudent to take on a short-term debt to get a business off the ground, but
only if you don't jeopardize the security of your family.

Debt is inviting from a distance, but the closer it comes, the more you can
see it is covered with warts. Do not become too familiar with debt and think you
must have it. It can be a ruthless master. It lacks compassion and does not care
about you or your family. Here's a comforting fact: You do not have to worry
about repaying debt if none has been incurred. If you have debt, pay it back. You
are no different from a conscienceless world if you easily default to bankruptcy.
Anyone can walk away from responsibility, but what a testimony doing the right
thing is. Creditors and friends will be amazed and even drawn to God through
your financial faithfulness. At the very least you will please God and will be able
to sleep well at night. Do not be overwhelmed by the overall amount of your
debt. Just be concerned about paying back what is owed today and trust God for
tomorrow. Indeed, one of the biggest reasons to avoid debt is so that you can
become a generous giver.

Generous giving is also a matter of financial faithfulness. It is a trust issue.
You really can increase your giving in the face of greater financial obligations.
This is God's economy. The greater your needs, the more your giving may need
to increase. It does not make sense, humanly speaking, and it could even be
construed as irresponsible. But, in fact, generosity is being responsible. It is
through generosity that our faith is tested and refined. If we give according to
how we can make the math work, then we miss a faith opportunity. Our faith
grows most when we are generous. And generosity is not defined by amount. It is
defined by motive and capacity. A dollar given by faith with a capacity of two

"He who walks with the wise grows wise, but a companion of fools suffers harm." Proverbs 13:20

Dose 30

dollars is radical faith, while a dollar given with a capacity of ten dollars is minimal faith. Often givers are the best fundraisers. People want to give toward generosity. So do not let your modest income and small net worth limit your giving. A generous giver is a generous giver, regardless of the gift size. Generosity starts where you are, not where you want to be. If God can trust you with a small amount of money, then He can trust you with a lot. The more you hold what you have with an open hand, the more you can be trusted.

Lastly, we can be generous givers and generous livers because of the debt of gratitude we owe God. Of course we can never pay Him back for the great love He has bestowed on us, but we can imitate His giving. There is no greater compliment than imitation. He gives to the undeserving. He gives to the ungrateful. He gives to the unsuspecting. He gives generously, lavishly and hilariously. Generous giving is His nature, and the very nature of God lives in your life through Jesus Christ. Simply put, be who you are. Be a generous giver, because He first gave and still gives to you. You can't outgive Him, but you can certainly join Him in this great adventure of generosity. Financial faithfulness is freedom!

God's Part

God looks with favor upon a heart of faith, but it's hard to have faith and depend on debt at the same time.

My Part

_____

_____

_____

_____

Pride's Presumption

"Do not go up, because the Lord is not with you. You will be defeated by your enemies.... Nevertheless, in their presumption they went up toward the high hill country, though neither Moses nor the ark of the Lord's covenant moved from the camp....[Their enemies] who lived in that hill country came down and attacked them and beat them down...."
Numbers 14:42, 44-45b

Pride presumes. It presumes on people and, more disturbingly, it presumes on God. It manipulates on behalf of "my" agenda. When you and I presume, we take matters into our own hands. Presumption is a big price to pay for forced results. You can do just about anything if you have enough time, money and will power. But, is this really the will of God? Do you really want to do this, or are your motives a product of your pride—presuming that the good times will keep on rolling? Everything you touched in the past may have turned to gold, but past success cannot justify future presumption. Instead, stay sharp and dependent on God.

When you first started out, there was a respect and dependence on God that defined you daily. Don't lose this. When you slip from dependence on God to presuming on God, you are set up for failure. God will not be used. This is not His style or the style of discerning leaders. Indeed, before you charge ahead, make sure others are up to speed and on board. You may artificially bend another's will, but eventually your subtle presumption of their loyalty will break their spirit and drive them away. They will not be taken for granted. It is a matter of respect. Will we respect the wishes of others, or will we plow ahead with a wake of relational wreckage behind us? Certain assumptions need to be questioned. The team that served you with excellence up until now may not be the team that takes you to the next level. Or, you may be the one who needs to be replaced. Do not presume that your level of leadership skills has the capacity to carry on the expansion of the enterprise. Presumption is painful and painstaking. Avoid it at all costs.

Presumption on God is the most serious derivative of pride. Religious pride subtly uses God to manipulate people and circumstances. It is sad but true. If left unchecked, God gets saddled with our immature goals and desires. Sometimes the desired outcome is noble, but the timing is unwise. A building program is a worthy goal, but it becomes presumption if the last facility is unpaid for and the future one needs to be highly leveraged by debt. Don't drag God into poor plan-

"He who walks with the wise grows wise, but a companion of fools suffers harm." Proverbs 13:20

Dose 31

ning and ask Him to bless it after the fact. Scripture is the Word of God. However, if a Bible verse is ripped from its context to prove a point of presumption, then it becomes a facilitator of deception. Do not use the Holy Bible for worldly outcomes. You cannot presume that the Scripture supports your desires just because it seems right. Emotion can lead you down the dead-end road of presumption.

Therefore, keep pride's presumption in check with humility's trust. Humility trusts God to come through without having to mandate or manipulate. Humility is patient to wait on people. You can have a sense of eternal urgency without being disrespectful or demanding. Pride will drive you ahead in presumption, without fear of God as a check and balance. Humility first seeks out the Lord in a quiet spot and listens for His voice of validation. Pride will push you to presume. Humility will invite you to trust. Trust God's promises, but do not presume that He will bless your pride. Pride's presumption will lead to your downfall. Humility's trust will lead to your success. Therefore, take a step back, wait, pray, listen and make sure the Lord is with you!

God's Part

When God speaks, He intends to be heard and obeyed. When He speaks, it's always for our instruction and benefit. He never wants us to presume His intention when He hasn't spoken.

My Part

_____

_____

_____

_____

_____

Scriptural Validation

"Now the Bereans were of more noble character than the Thessalonians, for they received the message with great eagerness and examined the Scriptures every day to see if what Paul said was true."
Acts 17:11

Even the message of respected Bible teachers needs to be validated by Scripture. This validation affirms them and causes the recipient to cultivate good habits of study. The process of Scriptural validation is as much for the hearer as it is for the speaker. A submitted student of Scripture is not trying to poke holes in an argument with a condescending attitude. If this is the case, he has missed the point of searching the Scripture for truth.

The reason you seek to validate a message from Scripture is for edification and evangelism. You are not the Scripture police. Rather your knowledge of Scripture becomes an invitation for others to discover truth. Deep down they desire the truth about God and the truth about themselves. So, do not be sloppy with your stewardship of Scriptural knowledge. Use your reservoir of truth prayerfully and with humility. Yes, challenge teachers, but do it in the spirit of a fellow learner and for their edification.

Also, make sure that your Scriptural understanding is constantly engaging outsiders in meaningful conversation. There's no need to talk down to or be intimidated by another's self-centered worldview. Rather, with patience and care listen intently. Bring them back to the person of Jesus. Paint for them a scriptural portrait of Jesus that cannot be denied. It is accurate and true because it is validated by Scripture. Scripture can hold its own—it just needs to be exposed. Remember that many are walking in darkness. They need a gradual illumination of Scripture like a developing photo in a dark room. Watch the chemical of questions and convictions bring about clearer understanding as the picture of truth continues to develop. Do not rush the process, and do not be timid as well. Indeed, lead people to read and validate the Scripture for themselves. As a result, evangelism and edification will explode from its pages. The shrapnel of truth will lodge in their heads and hearts. God changes lives through Scripture's validation.

Lastly, allow Scripture to validate your worldview. Do not take for granted what is presented as truth in your everyday life. For instance, your faith is not to be compartmentalized. Instead, your faith should weave throughout the fabric of

"He who walks with the wise grows wise, but a companion of fools suffers harm." Proverbs 13:20

Dose 32

your life. It is not a wise or accurate worldview that locks your faith away, only to be released on Sunday. This is an insult to God. Compartmentalization of your faith prostitutes your faith. Therefore validate all of your beliefs and behaviors by Scripture.

What you believe about money, marriage, work, parenting, relationships, government, business, international affairs, social issues and church all require a consistent worldview. If there is inconsistency, your behavior becomes erratic. Culture and feelings will validate your beliefs and behavior rather than Scripture. This lazy living is reactionary and ridiculous to God.

Therefore, start today to filter your faith through Scripture. Validate your actions or lack of action by Scripture. Then your life will become different. Others will take notice. You will become a lightning rod for evangelism and edification—a person of noble character!

God's Part

The only truth that we know is found in God's Word, and God declares that our study of it is profitable for every situation.

My Part

_____

_____

_____

_____

_____

Thirsty Soul

"As the deer pants for streams of water, so my soul pants for you, O God. My soul thirsts for God, for the living God. When can I go and meet with God?"
Psalm 42:1-2

A thirsty soul comes from God, and a thirsty soul is satisfied by God. This is how He has wired us. He designed us spiritually like He has designed us physically. We are dependent on forces outside of ourselves for satisfaction. There are not many sensations that cause a more desperate feeling than a craving for water. And, on the contrary, there are few things more refreshing than ice cold water on a hot and sultry summer day. When your body is depleted of fluids from physical exertion, it screams out for some relief. If you continue in this state of heat exhaustion, you will collapse from dehydration.

Our soul behaves the same way. We run through life hurried and empty. Our heated up emotions and our thirsty soul cries out for relief, but we continue to plow through the days without stopping for God. Our busyness of life turns into barrenness of soul. The energy is gone, the joy is depleted and our gratitude account is overdrawn. We have hit a wall and, as a consequence, spiritual dehydration occurs.

Then, as a necessity we are forced to get time with God. It may happen through illness, depression, divorce or the loss of a job, but why wait for a crisis to force us to God? He is available now. He is available daily—even moment by moment—to satisfy the longing of your soul. Soul thirst will never go away. It is one of God's built-in mechanisms of dependency. Wise is the man or woman who drinks often from God's wellspring of living water. We need at least a "gallon" of God each day. Yet, if the truth be known, we haphazardly splash down a cup of God like an out-of-shape runner battling up a long and treacherous hill.

How refreshing it is to sit by the banks of God's stream of living water. His water is wet, cool and refreshing. Life can be like a blistering sun. It beats down on you and, at times, you feel uncovered without a hat or sunglasses. God, on the other hand, provides shade and protection. He invites you to be still, listen and wait on Him. Let His Word feed your soul with a balanced diet of commands, encouragement and praise. Listen intently to His voice through prayer.

Dose 33

He loves you and He wants to tell you this often. Jesus satisfies. The world offers satisfaction but fails miserably. Its offer is a farce, a great deception. Jesus is simple and direct. "Drink of me," He says, "and you will never thirst again." What a promise! The satisfying Jesus is there for the taking. The longing within your soul is for Him. He wants to be your best friend. Let Him satisfy you first. Satisfaction is not from Jesus plus something else. It is not Jesus plus work, money or play. Satisfaction is Jesus alone.

Date Jesus. Put Him on your calendar. You calendar priorities. Make Jesus a priority and then keep your commitment. Meet with Him often. This is His heart and passion. He wants to satisfy your soul. Jesus is the great satisfier. You "can't get no satisfaction" outside of Christ. Drink often from the well of God. Draw deep from His waters. Let Christ quench your thirsty soul!

God's Part

The longing of the human soul is designed by God to lead us to Him.

My Part

_____

_____

_____

_____

_____

_____

Right Results, Wrong Methods

"The Lord said to Moses...speak to that rock....Moses said to them,
'Listen you rebels, must we bring you water out of this rock?' Then Moses
raised his arm and struck the rock twice with his staff. Water gushed out....
But the Lord said to Moses and Aaron, 'Because you did not trust in me to
honor me as holy in the sight of the Israelites, you will not bring this
community into the land I give them.'"
Numbers 20:7-8a, 10b, 12

Right results are not the measurement of success.

How you arrive at the results is even more important. It is not all about results. Of course results are important, done the right way. Pragmatism is not king. Christ is King. Christ cares as much or more about our methods as He does about our results. He may even bless our bad attitude in the short term, but He still requires our confession and repentance. A bad attitude leads to wrong methods. There is no getting around this. You cannot lower yourself to lash back at the ingratitude and immaturity of others. Cool off and pray before you angrily give them what they want. If you cave in to coercion, then you are a good candidate for doing the right thing the wrong way. Then you may remorsefully get the right results and bypass the use of wise methods.

This can happen as easily at home as at work. Do not blow up at your children and give them their way just because they whine and complain. This is a recipe for rebellion in their teenage years. Early on they learn how to manipulate your emotions. Indeed, an environment of fatigue and frustration is not conducive to wise decision making, and it is certainly not the best time to execute your decisions. Anger is like a large, dull knife. It gets results, but the process is jagged and bloody. Before you launch off into a direction of leadership, make sure that you have a defined process of wise methods and accurate measurements. Create these out of a calm and cool head. Do not act in a way that you later will regret. Previously planned processes are in place for your protection. These are checks and balances to assure excellence in execution.

God is very interested in our methods. He expects to be honored and respected in the process of getting results. If you run over people to reach your goal, it is an inaccurate reflection of the Lord you serve. However, if you serve people in the process of reaching the agreed-upon goal, you illustrate the heart of Jesus. So much hinges on our spirit, attitude and actions. This is a trilogy that

Dose 34

reflects right methods. Yes, methods need to be modified for efficiency and effectiveness, but this can be done through dialogue, not dictating. People are respected when the rationale is explained around a change in procedures. Of course, the best ideas can come from those responsible to implement them. Listen keenly to the voice of reason. Wisdom resides here.

You do not have to rush to get results out of fear. You can wait, pray and define a planned out process that is derived from collaboration with the team. Then your work is sustainable, and everyone is honored in the process. Focus on the right methods, and the right results will take care of themselves. Always remind yourself of how Christ would behave. It is the spirit of Jesus that cultivates the right attitudes and actions. Trust and honor God with the process and in the process. Then, the right methods will support the right results!

God's Part

God can produce results from nothing; He desires that His children would focus on methods that will honor Him.

My Part

_____

_____

_____

_____

_____

Holy Spirit Restraint

*"Paul and his companions traveled throughout the region of Phrygia
and Galatia, having been kept by the Holy Spirit from preaching the word
in the province of Asia."*
Acts 16:6

Sometimes the Holy Spirit restrains you. This may seem
weird and counterproductive. Your conflict of emotion comes when He restrains
you from something good. It is easy to understand His restraint from doing
drugs, online pornography, unwise financial decisions and unhealthy relationships; but why would the Holy Spirit keep you from a benevolent act? After all,
your good works are an outflow of God's love working through your heart. Your
motive is to please and obey Him.

However, the more you pray about it the more He confirms a "no" to this
good opportunity. Yes, God can say no to serving as an international missionary.
He can say no to a marriage with this particular godly person. He can say no to
the school you always dreamed of attending. You can't totally explain it, but He is
restraining you from accepting the best job offer you have ever received. But do
not despair, the Holy Spirit's restraint is what is best for you. It may be His
protection. It may be that He is preparing you for the next better person or
opportunity.

Do not get caught up in the euphoria of having to have this particular relationship, thing or job. Be willing to walk away at any time. This is wise stewardship of your time, money and abilities. What God had you invest in yesterday,
He may lead you to cease today for a better opportunity tomorrow. Yes, the Holy
Spirit many times leads you forward in a clear-cut direction. But, there are times
He will put things on hold. It is like time is suspended for the moment. You can
use this time of His restraint mode to invigorate your faith. Be glad, not mad or
sad. He is still using you. Though many questions still loom, He can still be
trusted.

Trust is the apex of activity on behalf of God. Following God is a great
adventure of faith. The Holy Spirit is your guide on this sometimes fearful, but
exhilarating experience in trust. It is like snaking your way down an uncharted
remote river through the wilderness of Idaho. You can only see what is on this
side of the bend. What is around the corner may be wrought with rapids and
rocks, but you trust your seasoned guide to anticipate any change or danger. He

"He who walks with the wise grows wise, but a companion of fools suffers harm." Proverbs 13:20

Dose 35

is the one who makes the call to stop or to move forward, or even to carry your raft over dry land to make it more efficiently to the next destination. Like this guide, the role of the Holy Spirit is to stop us or to move us forward. He will replace His no with a better yes. However, His no may seem final until gradually He reveals a new and better option. Trust Him with this no that seems hard for now. Life in retrospect will make much more sense.

Do not let the Holy Spirit's restraint keep you from doing the things you know are right. Stay engaged in discipleship and evangelism. Be the best parent or friend ever. Do not let this life detour deter you from going deeper with Christ. The Holy Spirit's restraint is not meant to keep you from the other 90% that you know to be God's will. Celebrate what He has done and will do through you. Let go of this missed opportunity or unmet expectation. What He has next for you may be better than you ever dreamed possible. You may not be thinking big enough. His no is a great time to pray for a bigger yes. Do not sell yourself or God short. Watch His will unfold with humility and faith. Trust Him that less may be more and more may be less. Restraint can be good, especially when the Holy Spirit is your restrainer!

God's Part

God knows best: He desires our trust, not always our understanding.

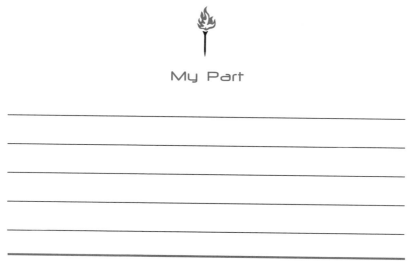

My Part

_____

_____

_____

_____

_____

Useless Money

*"Of what use is money in the hand of a fool,
since he has no desire to get wisdom?"*
Proverbs 17:16

Money is useless in the hands of a fool. Unfortunately, one who is a fool probably does not buy into this line of thinking. The fool sees money as a panacea. The fool wants the authority of managing money without the responsibility of its wise use. His solution is to throw more money toward a problem or a person in need when, in reality, the investment of more money in a bad situation prolongs the poor results.

Entrusting money to a fool is like giving the keys of your new car to a small child. There is initial excitement and enthusiasm, but after just a few driving episodes there is loss. There is the loss of value to the automobile because of the damage inflicted to its body. There is the loss of time needed to repair the car and the property of others involved in the mayhem. This is just the beginning. If unchecked, the losses continue to mount up. Money in the hands of a fool is a disaster waiting to happen. Its irresponsible use is like leaving a larger-than-life, handcrafted ice sculpture on the beach. In the beginning it is beautiful for all to admire but, as the sun beats down, it melts away into the hot and dry sand never to be seen again.

Money in the hands of a fool evaporates. It is dangerous for him and for those around him. The character flaws that were dormant or harmless pre-wealth become exacerbated post-wealth. Anger and pride rise up to dominate and control others with their newfound power through money. However false and fleeting the power may be, fools bask in admiration gained from other fools. Yes, fools with money attract other fools. It is a love feast of sorts, destined for waste in worldly activities. Money for the fool is all about today. It is all about squandering it on oneself and useless forays. Fools cannot handle money. Money ensnares a fool into bondage. Indeed, the wise are careful not to feed a foolish, irresponsible appetite.

The wise steward of money looks for other wise individuals, organizations and environments in which to invest God's resources. There is no real consideration to squander God's blessings on those who do not understand or appreciate God's game plan. So as you consider investing, invest with those very skilled in

"He who walks with the wise grows wise, but a companion of fools suffers harm." Proverbs 13:20

Dose 36

money's growth and in preservation of capital. Invest with those wise in the ways of God, who value what you value. With regards to giving, look for wise ministry leaders and boards who request accountability and are committed to financial integrity. We all do better when others are looking. Give to Kingdom-minded ministry organizations that submit and listen to godly counsel. Structure your gift so that it keeps on giving after you go to heaven.

Lastly, as it relates to inheritance, let all involved know that your motivation is for the Kingdom of God, not for the prince of this world. Structure your inheritance for others in a way that facilitates wisdom and responsibility. Obviously, it comes down to the choice of the inheritor to accept or reject this catalyst toward Christ-centered living. Prayerfully attempt to influence as many wise people as you can and avoid the foolish. Fools do not desire wisdom. Pray for an epidemic of desire toward the wise use of money. God will smile, others will be blessed and the Kingdom of God will be advanced. Be wise!

God's Part

God promises to bless and multiply money wisely invested into His Kingdom.

My Part

_____

_____

_____

_____

_____

Power of the Path

*"I [the angel of the Lord] have come here to oppose you because your path
is a reckless one before me."*
Numbers 22:32b

The path you choose is the path you use. It may be a path
of pride or a path of humility. The path may stimulate purity or impurity. It
could be a path of wisdom or a path of foolishness. The path may be one of
cooperation or a path of independence. Your path may be family friendly or
hostile to the health of your home. Be careful how you seek after success, because
you can easily veer down the path of lost accountability.

The path you choose is the path you use, so be very wise about the choices
you make. Make sure that the path you traverse follows through the woods of
God's will. Your path is a picture of overlaid choices. One after another, your
daily decisions dig out a well-beaten path. But, do not be deceived—every path
leads somewhere. Your current path is not insignificant. If it is a path of preparation, then prepare well. A well-prepared path paves the way for opportunity. Do
not complain about the limitations of your circumstances when you have not
been a good steward of your resources, relationships, finances and skills.

Choose the path of patient preparation. The more you prepare, the wider
this path becomes. The less you prepare the narrower it becomes. The path of
preparation may seem long and onerous at times, but be patient and stay the
course. Your faithfulness now will bolster your influence later. The path of preparation requires persevering patience. Travel this path with focused attention.
Enjoy the journey, for these may be the simplest days of your life. The path of
preparation is the strong foundation of any excellent and eternally significant
endeavor.

Another path to walk wisely upon is the path of personal intimacy with
God. It is easy to overlook this path because of familiarity or busyness. But, without a worn-out path to God, you will wear out. It is a path that requires discipline, but the fruit of your faith's exercise will serve you throughout life. When
you walk the path of intimacy with God, He fills you with His peace, security
and hope. This is not a path of quick fixes; rather, it is one of trust and
endurance.

Dose 37

Traveling a path without God is like walking in the country on a moonless night. Or, it is like running through a city during the day—blindfolded. In either case there is a lot of activity, but the activity is filled with fear, confusion, misdirection and eventual hurt. Indeed, the path of God is not without pain or uncertainty. But, as you travel on His path, you are filled with His presence. The presence of God is peaceful. It is purifying and pleasing to the soul. Moreover, life in itself is one big path. If you travel alone, it is daunting but, with Christ, it is edifying. The path of Christ is bumpy at times, but His freedom is exhilarating.

As you travel with God, be ever mindful of His guardrails of grace, love and law. They are there for your protection. They keep you from straying off His path of kingdom purpose. The worldly road most traveled is reckless compared to the less traveled path of heaven's security. Choose daily the wise path of confession and consultation with your creator. The path of obedience to God leads to peace with God. He is a friend to be admired, and a friend to be feared. Allow His opposition to lead you back down His path. His path is what's best. Travel it with Him and travel it for Him!

God's Part

Only God knows the destinations of the paths that He chooses for His children to follow, but the ultimate destination is always Himself.

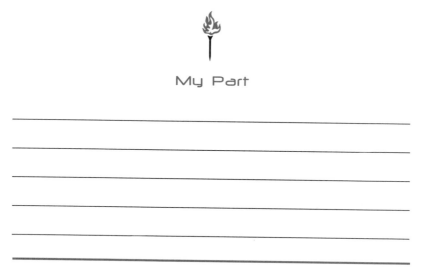

My Part

_____

_____

_____

_____

_____

Holy Spirit Compelled

"And now, compelled by the Holy Spirit, I am going to Jerusalem,
not knowing what will happen to me there."
Acts 20:22

Sometimes you are compelled by the Holy Spirit. It is an undeniable and internal call to move forward in faith. You may not even know the complete details of what will follow in the future. In fact, you probably will not understand completely what God is up to, but you follow Him anyway, trusting that He knows best. To be compelled by the Holy Spirit means you must do it. In your heart you know you will be disobedient if you do not follow this new and sometimes uncertain direction. It is exciting and scary at the same time.

However, these simultaneous emotions need not deter you; rather, use this newfound energy to accelerate your faith to the next level. This clarity in direction is what you have been seeking God about in sometimes broken and tearful petitions. So, if He is compelling you to attend graduate school, go for it. If He is compelling you to have another child, then say yes to this new opportunity for life. If He is urging you to give at new faith-stirring levels of your time and money to His Kingdom, then move quickly. There may be one country overseas where He is calling you to be a lightning rod of Kingdom transformation. Do not shrink back with fear and trepidation. Instead, trust Him with the resources and the relationships that will rise to the occasion. Your increase in faith will do the same for others.

Where the Holy Spirit leads, He produces results way beyond your ability to accomplish the same. Indeed, your new destination may not be a safe place. It may even be hostile to you and what you stand for. However, God can still be trusted. The seeds of your service will not go unattended by the Holy Spirit. He waters, cultivates and harvests where the Word of God has been planted and nurtured. A life compelled by Christ is courageous and content!

You are "in the zone" when you are compelled by the Holy Spirit. This is a window of opportunity that cannot be denied. Seize this God-moment. You will look back and be amazed that the Holy Spirit chose you for this eternal endeavor. The humility and gratitude will drive you to your knees in praise and adoration for your heavenly Father's blessing beyond measure. This is the fruit of a Holy Spirit-compelled life lived by faith. You become a man or woman overwhelmed

Dose 38

by the goodness and greatness of God. Your love for people is extraordinary because you have been loved by God in His supernatural manner. The Holy Spirit compels you to more life-changing results on earth because you are more surrendered in obedience to heaven's agenda. This compelling drama is beautiful and fun to watch.

A life compelled by the Holy Spirit cannot be stopped. Death may cause the body to cease from functioning, but the influence remains and may even intensify. Wow! Wooed by the Holy Spirit! Called by the Holy Spirit! And compelled by the Holy Spirit! Life is too short to not live with this compelling vision and tension. It is the tension of living by faith in Christ. Follow the Holy Spirit's compelling lead. He is with you and for you. He is at your destination in His revealing power. Do not recoil from this rendezvous with radical faith and obedience!

God's Part

The push of God is awe-inspiring and life-changing—whether it's a push out of the "nest" of comfort and familiarity or a push into a rushing stream of nonstop ministry. He knows what He's doing; He can be trusted.

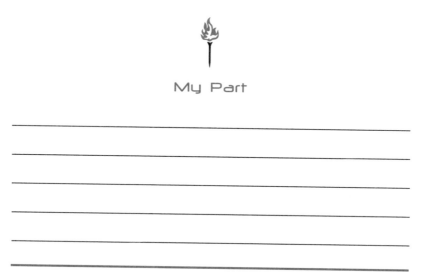

My Part

_____

_____

_____

_____

_____

_____

Confession's Cleansing

"Have mercy on me O God, according to your unfailing love; according to your great compassion blot out my transgressions. Wash away all my iniquity and cleanse me from my sin."
Psalm 51:1-2

Confession is cleansing. It is coming clean with God. Our hearts become soiled over time and need purifying. A dirty heart is not unlike the engine of a well-driven car. The shiny washed and waxed hood can cover an engine that is baked with road film, grime and grease. The responsible and conscientious car owner may have his car detailed. This precise process cleans every nook and cranny of the car.

Our hearts need the same. We need an ongoing detail job. We need God to bring back the newness of our faith and the freshness of our sensitivity to sin. The opposite of a cleansed heart is a hardened heart. We become hardened to humility. We become hardened to honesty. We become hardened to change. We become hardened to learning. We become hardened to people. And, worst of all, we become hardened to God. This is a hard way to live. On the other hand, we can take responsibility for our sin and agree with Him about its hideous presence in our lives.

Confession is agreeing with God on what is right and wrong. It is admitting to the violation of one or the other of His commands and then coming clean with Him. Confession is coming to grips with what God already knows. Confession is not new information to God, but it does remove walls of pride that we build up. Pride is a reason for unconfessed sin. We do not want to admit we are wrong. Confession punctures our "pride balloon." However this is exactly what needs to happen. Pride needs to be deflated and replaced with humility. There are many benefits to confession, and this is just one of them.

Confession lifts guilt and gives you a jolt of joy. Oh the freedom of a clear conscience! You do not have to rack your brain in remembrance of past offenses that you continue to cover up. Your energy is freed to sow righteousness rather than try to keep a lid on sin. Unconfessed sin will not go away. It will come out one way or another. It may manifest itself in your health and or your attitude, but it will not remain hidden. The greatest benefit of confession is reengagement with God. What a lonely place it is to be estranged from your heavenly Father.

Dose 39

He is waiting for you throughout each day to turn to Him and set the relationship straight. A fractured friendship with your best friend can be deeply painful. Confession begins the relational healing process. Confession to God may lead to confession with people. Sometimes this is harder because certain people may not forgive you. However, your confession to another may free them to do the same.

Confession is disarming. It gives others the freedom to open up and not fear condemnation. Confession gives you the moral authority to mentor, lead, parent and teach others. Your posture becomes one of weakness and dependence on God and people, instead of prideful power and the cover up of sin. Confession is healing. The wounds, sometimes deep wounds, that you have unknowingly inflicted or received begin to heal with the ointment of confession. Come clean today with God and others. Then, watch the power of confession draw you closer to God and closer to people!

God's Part

Only God, in His mercy and grace, can fully forgive sin—He promises never to cast out the penitent, confessing soul.

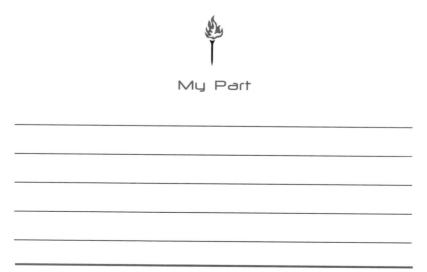

My Part

_____

_____

_____

_____

_____

Succession Planning

"Moses said to the Lord, 'May the Lord, the God of the spirits of all mankind, appoint a man over this community to go out and come in before them, one who will lead them out and bring them in, so the Lord's people will not be like sheep without a shepherd."
Numbers 27:15-17

Succession planning begins with prayer. It is a divinely directed process through which God leads those responsible to select the successor. It may be a board of directors in a business or a board of elders in a church, but they both need the attention of the Almighty. Providence has a stellar track record of anointing the next-generation leaders. A God-ordained leader has what it takes to serve the enterprise with clarity and credibility. Your role as the current leader is to work yourself out of your job.

If you are growing and learning, there will always be new and challenging opportunities to stretch and grow your abilities. Avoid becoming a creature of comfort with no room for change and transition. It is during the times of change and added responsibility that you learn the most. Leadership matures in the fires of advancement, not in the ease of maintaining. Who are you grooming as your successor? The reality is, your apprentice will probably do a better job than you. The organization requires a different skill set for this season of expansion. Your fingerprints are evident on everyone, from the maintenance crew to the board room.

Your influence will be felt for some time to come. But, now is the time to lengthen your legacy with younger leadership. Youth is the lifeblood of keeping the vision alive. Youth brings energy, innovation and entrepreneurship. Embrace their new way of doing things. This is how you and the enterprise will stay relevant and competitive in the marketplace. Pray for God to send your way a young-at-heart leader, full of the Holy Spirit, who is gifted and skilled to take the mission of the organization to the next level. Indeed, you may not have to search very far.

Succession is also good stewardship. If things fall apart after you leave, it is a very poor reflection of your leadership. Instead of empowering and equipping thoughtful leaders, you failed to enable people to reach their potential. Great leaders grow leaders. Poor leaders stunt the growth of leaders. Look at your succession plan as a budget of time, money and training. You have a window of

Dose 40

opportunity to impact the next generation by how well you choose and train your successor. Do not leave this as a problem for others, who will have to pick up the pieces after you leave. Involve your board, trusted advisors and management team early in the process. Shepherd two to three great candidates through a comprehensive prequalification process. Observe how they treat their spouses, restaurant servers and your least recognized team members. Look for respect to reign in their attitudes toward all types of people.

Finally, then, make a selection of someone with success at home, at work, at church and in the community. God's plan requires succession. It can be abrupt, or it can be a prayerful and thought-through process. The latter has a greater chance for success. And you, the one being replaced, need to disengage yourself after your replacement officially comes on board. You bless and commission your successor; then you leave. This is what is best for everyone. Great succession planning hangs on to security in God and lets go of influence at work. Effective succession has to be given before it can be received. The capstone of your career hinges on your ability to hand off. Success is in your successor. Trust the Lord with His appointee!

God's Part

Any God-ordained enterprise will never lack a successful leader provided God is allowed to make the selection.

My Part

_____

_____

_____

_____

Ministry Leadership

*"Leaving the next day, we reached Caesarea and stayed at the house
of Philip the evangelist, one of the Seven. He had four unmarried
daughters who prophesied."*
Acts 21:8-9

As followers of Jesus Christ we are all called to ministry. Your life
is your ministry. Your work is your ministry. Your home is your ministry. Your
children are your ministry. Your parents are your ministry. Everything about you
has ministry implications. However, God calls some to ministry leadership.
Ministry leadership may mean ministry as a career calling, but God's call to
ministry leadership does not mean you have arrived in your spiritual maturity.

On the contrary, you are still a work in process. There is an expectation for
your ongoing growth in grace and faith in Jesus. You are called to be a model of
Christlike character for others to emulate and learn from. It is certainly no reason
for pride; rather, it calls for humility and dependence on God. Make sure that
you use your position of influence for the welfare of others and not yourself. You
have been given a trust that is very, very valuable. Ministry leadership lends itself
to respect and influence. This respect can be channeled into acts of service, influence on unbelievers and the encouragement of believers.

Your responsibility as a leader in ministry begins at home. Do not be
surprised that as you serve your family with humility and grace, your children
will follow God's call to ministry leadership. In some ways this can be expected,
but it is certainly not required, much less demanded. Hold your children's future
and career callings with an open hand. Their zeal for ministry leadership overseas,
with teenagers at home, or in the local ghettos may be for a season or for a lifetime. This is between them and God. Your opinion as a parent is important on
how and where they should serve, but ultimately they answer to God.

Are you uncomfortable with your child becoming a ministry leader? Why? Is
it because it does not pay well or because you think they can do better in a career
choice, or both? Is it a blow to your own ego? You can relax. As a parent you can
practice what you preach. You have always believed that God's will is what is best
for everyone involved. This is a reassuring truth you can rest in. If your child is
called by God to serve internationally, then celebrate their opportunity to serve a
hurting world. Look forward to your own overseas travel to be with them and

Dose 41

experience a new and interesting culture. Do not let your pride and expectations discourage your son or daughter from being "full time" in the faith. If he or she feels called to invest in college students during their waking hours, then encourage and support them in this eternal endeavor. Do not remain stoic and passive in your support. What you don't say sometimes speaks louder than what you do say. Help them financially. Volunteer. Facilitate resources and relationships that will contribute to their ministry leadership success. Rejoice that they are following hard after heaven and are not consumed with this world.

Your blessing of your child's choice of ministry leadership may be the very thing needed for them to be successful. Tell them how proud you are of them. Urge them to continue in ministry leadership empowered by the Holy Spirit. Ministry leadership is a legitimate and responsible call of God. Live it and encourage it!

God's Part

God lends us children as a fiduciary responsibility; they don't belong to us—they belong to Him. God expects us, as good stewards, to support His call on our children's lives.

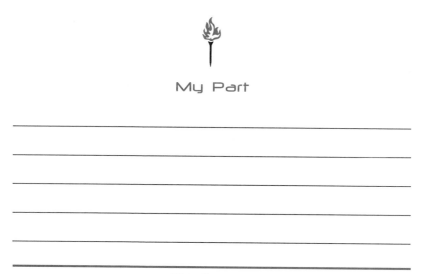

My Part

_____

_____

_____

_____

_____

_____

A Friend's Betrayal

"If an enemy were insulting me, I could endure it; if a foe were raising himself against me, I could hide from him. But it is you, a man like myself, my companion, my close friend, with whom I once enjoyed sweet fellowship as we walked with the throng at the house of God."
Psalm 55:12-14

Betrayal from a friend is crushing. It is confusing. Someone whom you thought was with you no matter what left when the going got rough. Your spouse was unfaithful. A close friend betrayed a confidence you had entrusted to him or her. An ex-employee stole your best client after agreeing to a two-year non-compete. Money is a leading cause for betrayal. Your friend left you "holding the bag" for more money. They sold out your friendship for wealth. They valued stuff more than they valued you. Judas betrayed Jesus for money.

This is universal and has been happening a long time, yet it still hurts. There is deep pain because a trust has been violated. You trusted this person with your family, with your money and with significant responsibilities at work. Even more significantly you trusted them with the secrets of your heart. You bore your soul to them unrestrained and unashamed. And they did the same. There was an authentic trust and loyalty both ways, or so it seemed. You dreamed together, vacationed together and worked together.

So what happened? It was probably a process. It probably did not happen overnight. And be careful how you define betrayal. Just because someone disengages from a relationship doesn't mean they are a traitor. It may be God's will for a change and a time for both parties to move on. That being said, there is something viler than human betrayal. The worst offense is to betray Jesus.

You once walked with Him in sweet fellowship. He was truly your best friend. But, over time, the relationship grew cool and distant. It "lost steam." Gradually you drifted over to the dark side. The allure of the world led you to separate from God. You may have become disillusioned because of bad things happening to good people. You may have become weary of trying to be a Christian. Or, other so-called Christians may have let you down and caused you to say, "If that is the way a Christian lives then I do not want to have anything to do with the church."

Betrayal of Christ can come in many forms and happen for a variety of

Dose 42

reasons. The good news is that you can repent from leaving Jesus and come back over from the enemy lines. You may have sold yourself to the enemy, but now you have awakened to reality. You do not have to stay in that perpetual state of guilt and confusion. You can come back home. The same Jesus you have betrayed is the same Jesus who will welcome you home. You can turn from the spiritual scraps the enemy has fed you in their prison camps and be set free to feast back with God at His table of grace. God is waiting for you to receive His love and acceptance. Jesus is empathic. He loves you right where you are. He has not given up on you, so don't give up on Him.

Betrayal cannot be the final word. Forgiveness and reconciliation is God's will, and you may need to do the same for someone else. Follow Christ's example by forgiving your betrayer and welcoming them back into your life. Ask them for forgiveness of your offenses, and trust God with the healing. Over time God can knit your hearts back together. Betrayal is ugly, but reconciliation is beautiful. Be beautiful!

God's Part

God always takes the initiative to restore broken fellowship—even the fellowship broken by betrayal—and He gives grace to His children to follow His example.

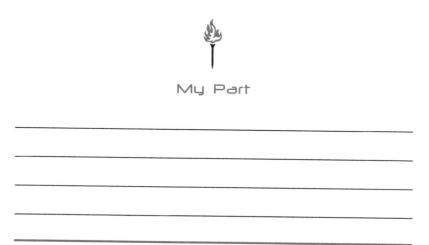

My Part

_____

_____

_____

_____

_____

God's Anger

"And here you are, a brood of sinners, standing in the place of your fathers and making the Lord even more angry with Israel. If you turn away from following him, he will again leave all this people in the desert, and you will be the cause of their destruction."
Numbers 32:14-15

God's anger is real. His angry side is as prevalent as His loving side. It is because of His anger that we appreciate His love. Without the wrath of God, we would not understand the grace of God. Our Lord without anger would be like a home security system unplugged and without power. It would look safe and impressive, but the reality of its protection would be void. There is no alarm, or security from harm and evil with a disengaged home security system.

The opposite can be said about our concerned and engaged heavenly Father. He becomes angry because He cares so much. His anger is for our protection. He only becomes angry around what is deeply valuable to Him. You are one of His precious ones. Your value to God is priceless. Indeed, He is extremely patient. However, His patience runs thin with our recurring sin and disobedience.

If you seek to take advantage of God's good grace, there will be consequences. You cannot snub the Lord's principles for living and not experience a painful backlash. God's grace without the consequences of sin is only a sentimental feeling. God's anger follows a life of sin and disrepair. He is seeking to get our attention in the middle of our negative results. Because He cares, He is relentless in His pursuit of you. Be grateful that His anger has finally grabbed your attention. Your life has been like a bad dream invoked by unwise choices. Now He has awakened you from your sinful slumber by a looming crisis. The death of a friend, a broken heart, a cruel illness, divorce, depression or bankruptcy—one or a combination of these has put you over the edge. God is angry at the injustice you are experiencing, and perhaps He is angry with you. So, now is the time to return to Him and to follow Him with your whole heart!

The anger of God subsides in the face of confession and repentance of sin. As your pride transforms to humility, God's grace and forgiveness extends beyond His anger. You may have even lashed back in anger in response to His. However, the anger of God cannot be compared to the anger of man. The Lord's anger is pure, holy and without sin. The anger of man is tainted by his sinful heart. You

Dose 43

can have a righteous anger, which comes from Christ living within you. But, Christ is not angry with Himself. His anger is directed at sin and those who promote its use. Channel your anger toward objects of God's anger, and you will experience a sinless anger. This is righteous indignation. Moreover, flee the wrath of God, by placing your faith in Christ. Trust Him for your salvation from hell in eternity and a hellish life on earth.

Wise choices lead to an abundant life on earth. This makes God smile. Don't push the envelope with God. He is not a passive grandfather who winks at your destructive indiscretions. Serve and love Him wholeheartedly. Do what He says. Follow the example and commands of Jesus. Therefore, you invite His affirmation and not His anger. We are much better off in the loving hand of God, than the angry hand of God. You can turn away from Him and follow your own way, but you will experience His displeasure. Or, you can turn to Him and follow Christ, and you will experience His pleasure!

God's Part

God is holy—entirely and completely—and cannot tolerate sin even for a second. The precious grace that He affords to sinners comes at a price—the atoning death of His Son.

My Part

_____

_____

_____

_____

_____

A Clear Conscience

"So I strive always to keep my conscience clear before God and man."
Acts 24:16

A clear conscience contributes to a good night's rest.

It is necessary to live at peace with God and man. A clear conscience is not final; rather it is an ongoing work. Therefore, make a conscious effort to keep a clear conscience. It is a test of honesty between God and me. Am I being truthful with respect to how I act in comparison to what I say I believe? If not, there will be a conflict that holds me back from experiencing God and life to its fullest. It is the fruit of a murky conscience. If not cleared up, there may very well be relational, spiritual, emotional, financial, and even physical consequences.

There is a high price to pay for an unclear conscience. What exactly is a clear conscience? A clear conscience means there is nothing between you and God or between you and another person. As best as you know, you have updated your relational account both with God and any other person. There are no sins of commission that need to be dealt with, and there are no sins of omission that are outstanding. Another contributor to conscience clutter can be money.

For example, you may be unable to pay your bills. Therefore, you may need to sell your home and use the equity in the house to come clean with your creditors. Rather than drown in debt, sell the house God has given you and thus receive His lifesaver of a clear conscience. Do not fight your own pride and ego. Trust God. Your obedience to what is right will pave the way for something better over the long run. Moreover, what value can you place on a clear conscience? It is one of the most valued assets you can own next to your salvation and your relational equity with others.

So, how can you cultivate a clear conscience? One key contributor to a clear conscience is the confession of and repentance from sin. You are prayed up, confessed up and cleaned up. In other words, no sin is dominating or controlling your life. This is why accountability is critical. You may be harboring sin and not know it. You may be living in a state of denial. Anger, resentment and bitterness can be masked very well. Left unattended you can spiral down into the depths of depression. This is where a community of caring friends can help you through this time of conscience conflict. Your wounded heart has never quite been healed by the grace of God. Your forgiveness toward another is not complete and

Dose 44

continual. But, when you slow down enough to be honest with yourself, this unforgiveness eats away at your conscience. Though you were the victim, you have remained a victim. And, even worse, you have become a victimizer. You will make victims of others unless you break this chain of wounded living. Victims need not stay there in perpetuity. A person with a victim mentality always has something gnawing at their psyche. Their conscience cannot rest because they have not forgiven. Jesus taught profoundly, "Unless you forgive others your father in heaven will not forgive you."

Forgiveness is the linchpin of a clear conscience. Your own forgiveness and your forgiveness of others are necessary to enjoy a clear conscience. Also, be aware of false guilt. This is a trick of the enemy to bog you down in the mire of self-imposed standards that are either unrealistic or unnecessary. Let your Holy Spirit-controlled conscience be your guide. A conscience that "marinates" in the Spirit's influence will be free and clear. Indeed, a clear conscience is going places!

God's Part

The job of God's Spirit is to engage the sinner's conscience to bring about true confession, repentance and victorious living.

My Part

_____

_____

_____

_____

_____

Excessive Talk

"A gossip betrays a confidence; so avoid a man who talks too much."
Proverbs 20:19

Not only is talk cheap, but too much of it can be lethal. Excessive talk can maroon a marriage, derail a deal, alienate close friends and offend acquaintances. Measured words are always the most meaningful. These wise nuggets are to be spent purposefully. Words are not designed to impress; rather, they are to encourage and instruct. We all fall into this trap from time to time. We want others to believe we are significant, so we use words to prove our point. Our words describe how much knowledge we have acquired, who we know, what we do, where we live, what we drive, where we have traveled and, of course, how great a family we have been blessed with.

If we are not careful, we can subtly (and not so subtly) hijack words for our own promotion and validation—especially as you dive into your relational portfolio. This requires as much discretion as if you were discussing your personal finances. Most people are forgiving until you disclose personal information. It doesn't matter if your disclosure is intentional or inadvertent. The results are the same—hurt and embarrassment. This personal trust is much more valuable than money.

Discretion needs to be in control of any discussion about anyone. Otherwise, you are flirting with gossip and the betrayal of a confidence. I struggle with this. My flesh wants recognition for the important people I know. After all, if you are impressed with my contacts and credentials, I will feel more valued and important. Or, in another scenario, you unwisely reveal confidential information in the form of a prayer request. You cannot wrap wrong actions around spiritual activities and language. This is doubly bad. This prayer should be for my discretion rather than my disclosure of juicy gossip. By God's grace correct this in your own life and avoid others who commit these same errors of indiscreet living.

Conversational etiquette can be learned. Even a silent fool is considered wise at times. Many times wisdom is found in what you don't say instead of what you do say. Word restraint is a sign of maturity. Yes, by all means be transparent but with a governor. Trust and confidentiality grow through experiences of faithfulness between parties. As discretion is demonstrated, more trust and information is given. When you find a confidant, you have found a good thing. Their lips are

Dose 45

sealed. Your stored information resides in the airtight vault of their heart and mind. They are there for you, not for themselves. They are secure in Christ and have no reason to prove anything to anyone. Not only do these treasured friends not gossip, they despise it in others. In fact, they are so bold as to interrupt a gossip in mid-sentence and ask them to cease before they make a fool of themselves.

Yes, we need to pray for others snared by sin or who are in a career free fall. And prayer for others means we talk with God. We posture ourselves humbly before God in heart and mind, crying out as their advocate. We ask for mercy, forgiveness, healing, restoration and reconciliation. It is an attitude of compassion and grace. We are willing to put our good name on the line for our hurting brother or sister in Christ. We talk to God on their behalf rather than to others for our benefit. This is one remedy for excessive talking: throttle back our words to people and increase our words to God. In essence, to avoid gossip and gossipers, talk more to God and less to people. Increase Jesus' words and decrease people's words. This is a word to the wise!

God's Part

God brings the needs and shortcomings of others to your attention for intercession and blessing, not for gossip.

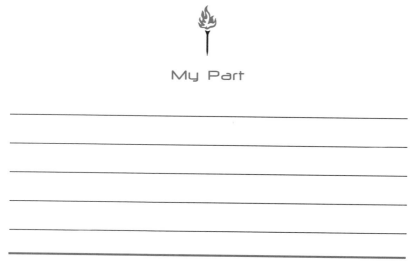

My Part

_____

_____

_____

_____

_____

Heart Test

"Remember how the Lord your God led you all the way in the desert these forty years, to humble you and to test you in order to know what was in your heart, whether or not you would keep his commands."
Deuteronomy 8:2

The treadmill of life can provide a real stress test for our heart. What's in our heart comes out under duress. If resentment resides in your heart, then anger appears. If forgiveness is found in your heart, then peace exudes when pressured by outside forces. The heart does not show its true colors until it faces a test. It is under the fire of a test that the heart of the matter surfaces to the top. This is why someone is able to mask hurt over a lifetime of disappointment by ignoring its deep-rooted influence. You can hide what's in your heart, but eventually a test will lure it out. And, its exposure is for your benefit.

God already knows what is concealed in your heart. He is waiting to unlock its motives so that you can pass or fail His test of obedience. None of us likes to fail a test. That brings a feeling of incompetence and, sometimes, stupidity. We fail tests for a variety of reasons. Maybe there was a misunderstanding of the assignment, or we were bored with the material, or we just chose to do other things rather than prepare. This can be true in our relationship with God as well. We can plead ignorance to God's commands and understanding His ways. But this is a poor excuse in light of the voluminous resources of His truth and teaching that is available to us all.

If boredom with the Christian life is an issue, you may need to discover, or rediscover, the real thing. Indeed, there is nothing about Jesus that is boring. Or, if you have delayed your spiritual preparation, then now is a good time to get started. It is never too late to fall in love with God, serve Him, and follow His ways. Your life experience is preparation for the Kingdom of Heaven. Therefore, engage with Christ in robust worship and intimate community with other followers of His.

Your current situation may very well be a test from God. He is squeezing your heart to see what is inside. It is healthy to flush out deceptive feelings that may be leading you to be fearful and to distrust. Your heart can be a tool of transformation for good, or it can be Satan's device of deception. Moreover, this test you are experiencing has jolted you into reality. You now have a desperate

Dose 46

and fresh dependence on God. He is front and center in your thinking. The carousel of careless living has stopped, and you are dizzy with despair. It is at this point of dependence on God where you need to camp out. Never leave this posture of prayer. He will meet you here every time.

Or, maybe this is a test of affluence. Your wealth has exceeded all limits and expectations. Will you stick to your guns of giving it all away beyond your cap of contentment? This is a test of what is truly in your heart. Words can easily betray what your heart's motivation really is, but your actions will validate their worth. Your prosperity can compete with your obedience to God, or it can accelerate it.

Use this heavenly test for the transformation of your earthly thinking. One reason that bad things happen to good people is to enable them to see what motivates them. A worthy motivation is nothing less than unleashing the character of Christ within your heart. Allow this test to recalibrate you and transform you to this standard. Tests are for a season. Tests are for a reason. Tests purify. Tests mature. Tests bless. Tests are for your good. Therefore, prepare, learn and test well for His glory!

God's Part

Only God knows what a person's heart contains—what truly motivates him or her. He shares that knowledge by way of testing.

My Part

_____

_____

_____

_____

_____

Show Up

"The brothers there had heard that we were coming, and they traveled as far as the Forum of Appius and the Three Taverns to meet us. At the sight of these men Paul thanked God and was encouraged."
Acts 28:15

Friends in trouble need us to show up. It is OK not to know what to say. Your presence speaks volumes. Just showing up many times causes people to thank God and be encouraged. They thank God because they see God in you. They see His care. They see His concern. They see His love. They see His compassion. Because Jesus lives in you, you are grace personified to a suffering saint. However, to meet a friend in faith at their point of need may require some inconvenience on your part. To encourage them in their misfortune may mean you have to rearrange your schedule and say no to something important but not necessary. Investments in people take time and sometimes sacrifice. People care can be messy. Cancer can be cruel. But when a friend is under its curse, then we can be there to bless.

Do not worry about what to say—just show up. Speak very little and when you do, ask sincere questions. Appropriate questions may be, "How can I help?" Or, "How can I pray for you and your family?" Or, a tender, "How do you feel?" No sermonizing or stories of people who suffered similar plights are edifying. Yes, weave in a prayer and soothing Scripture during your time, but do all with sensitivity to the Spirit's leading. Just showing up is the best medicine. Do not be concerned about your own feelings of inadequacies or sadness. Keep the focus on Christ and "loving on" your friend in need. You are God's deliverer of grace and kindness. "I do not do hospitals" is no excuse. Jesus said that hanging out with the sick was equivalent to ministering to Him. It is a journey with Jesus, on behalf of Jesus and to Jesus when you care for the hurting.

God may be calling you to travel a long distance to encourage a friend in the faith. Maybe the need is to travel overseas to a land and people ravished by poverty and disease. There may be Christians on the ground serving on foreign soil that need for you to show up. They do not need you to provide answers or pontificate about the plight of the people. What they need are loving leaders who will show up and who will serve under the leadership of the nationals at their point of perceived and real needs. Moreover, prison is the sentence of some. There are currently Christians who are incarcerated for their faith. They need our

Dose 47

encouragement and prayers. Pray that we who are free of jail can feel the pain of those who are locked up for Jesus. Public expression of faith is not to be taken for granted. Millions of believers around the globe cannot proclaim or discuss Christ publicly, yet the church is thriving in some of these faith-confining environments. When you show up there, be careful—you will be changed forever. The faith of the West looks fragile and fatigued compared to those saints' faith that has been galvanized by persecution.

So, show up—not just for the encouragement of the friend in need but for your own edification. You will go to be a blessing and in turn will receive much more of a blessing. This is how God works many times. The sufferers become the encouragers. Your gratitude to God explodes because of the faith and hope you witness in others suffering "mega" trials and tribulations. Show up to help others so that you, in turn, can be helped. We are a family of faith. We all need each other, especially in times like these!

God's Part

God knows what we need even before we ask, and He sends His servants to meet those needs—even if that means just "showing up."

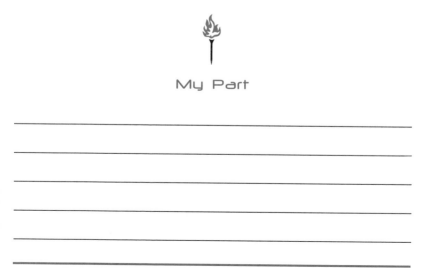

My Part

_____

_____

_____

_____

_____

Follow Through

"I will come to your temple with burnt offerings and fulfill my vows to you—
vows my lips promised and my mouth spoke when I was in trouble."
Psalm 66:13-14

Many times it is easier to make a promise than it is to keep a promise. This is why it is wise to be careful with our commitments. A good pattern is to under-promise and over-deliver. An unfulfilled promise leads to disappointment and loss of credibility, but follow-through brands you as one who keeps his word. You are mature and measured in how you use your words. Your motive is not to impress with rash promises, but rather to serve someone with a prayerful promise that is doable. A promise is a two-edged sword. If the promise is fulfilled, it is beneficial; if left unfulfilled, it is injurious.

Especially be cautious about the promises you make in the heat of emotion. Emotions may cause you to say strange things. Cool down, restore a level head, pray and seek counsel, then come back to the table with a practical commitment that has a high probability of follow-though. Indeed, you may need to go back to the one to whom you promised and ask for a reprieve or, at the very least, a modification that is more in line with your capacity. This requires a good dose of humility and eating of humble pie, but that's OK. Humility needs to drive promises in the first place.

Pride makes promises for the wrong reasons. Pride-driven promises are for the ego of the one making the promise. Or, a promise can be motivated as a response to guilt and trying to make up for lost time. Promises led by humility are prayerfully calculated and made for Christ's sake. Follow-through separates great people from good people, wise people from foolish people, professional people from unprofessional people and mature people from immature people.

A promise made to God is the most grave—this is a vow. A vow to God is an earnest promise to believe certain things or behave in a defined way. You may enter into a vow of poverty, a vow to abstain from sex outside of marriage, a vow to avoid alcohol and drugs, or a vow to run your business on biblical principles. It should go without saying that vows to God should not be made lightly. He remembers. There is no need for a written contract for His sake (maybe yours). It is easier to start the Christian life than it is to follow through in living the Christian life. Your salvation was a relief. You were rescued from yourself, sin,

"He who walks with the wise grows wise, but a companion of fools suffers harm." Proverbs 13:20

Dose 48

Satan and hell. Now it is time to work out your faith. There is follow-through needed to fulfill your vow with God. When we promised to follow Jesus, it meant we would follow wherever He led. We would trust Him regardless of the circumstances or challenges.

By the way, our marriage vows are not only a commitment to each other, but they are a promise to God. When there is marriage turmoil, you stick together because of your promise to God, each other and the Christian community. It is a matter of follow-through. Our promises to God are for our benefit. Remember what you told God you would do if He did something in particular for you. Follow up on this and then follow through.

The integrity of our word starts with God. When we do what we promised God, then it will be easier to follow through with our promises to people. Make fewer prayerful promises and by God's grace always follow through!

God's Part

God requires follow-through on our promises to Him and to others.

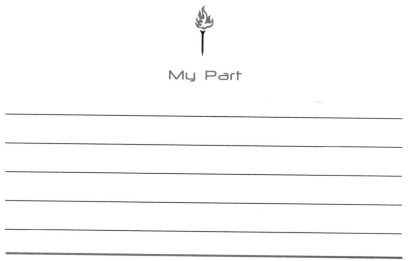

My Part

_____

_____

_____

_____

_____

Wealth's Source

*"You may say to yourself, 'My power and the strength of my hands have
produced this wealth for me.' But remember the Lord your God, for it is he
who gives you the ability to produce wealth, and so confirms his covenant,
which he swore to your forefathers, as it is today."*
Deuteronomy 8:17-18

God is the source of wealth. He has the ability to give it, and He
has the ability to take it. Wealth is not a result created by ourselves, but by Him.
We have skills, but He gave us the skills. We have intelligence, but He gave us
the intelligence. We have business acumen, but He gave us business acumen. We
work hard, but He gave us the drive and the health to work hard. Wealth's
creation and accumulation comes back to God. He is the "brains" behind the
operation. He gives us the abilities to produce wealth.

Whenever we forget this, we begin slipping down the slippery slope of pride
and self-sufficiency. Indeed, it was easier to depend on God when you had nothing. Now that you have more than you ever dreamed, it is tempting to not credit
King Jesus with your wealth and resources. He is not a silent or passive partner
with you. He is the owner of you and your assets. And as owner He deserves and
desires full disclosure of His powerful position.

Therefore, this does beg a very significant question. How does God expect
me to steward the wealth He has entrusted to me? Of course it is not the "bigger
barn" syndrome of lavishing all these resources on my wants and desires. Indeed,
a good place to start is with the poor. The poor are prevalent in unprecedented
numbers. However, their screams are silent, so they still lack the proper attention
God desires. The poor are mostly "out of sight," thus "out of mind," in the life of
the wealthy. But the heart of Christ breaks for the poor. His heart for the poor is
"top of mind." This is His desire for His followers. The poor do not deserve what
is left over. They deserve "first dibs." We need to direct our front line giving to
the poor and needy. Rub elbows with the poor, and you will give to the poor!

Wealth is a huge responsibility not to be taken lightly. If you take credit for
it, you have your reward. Your control of wealth without regard to God's heart
assures an earth-bound reward. However, wealth invested and given to heavenly
endeavors produces results and rewards way beyond this life. This is a promise of
God. Pride facilitates spiritual amnesia. The less needy you become, the more

Dose 49

you drift from your greatest source of need, Almighty God. In reality the more you have, the more you need God. You can only handle wealth well with God's guidance. Otherwise, you are too guarded by greed, obsessed with opulence, or faith-frozen by fear. God's guidance will free you through generosity and unleash you to pursue Kingdom initiatives.

So never forget that He is the source of your strength, the provider of your power, the wellspring of your wisdom, the artist of your abilities and the underpinning of your wealth. You remain "blessable" and blessed when you are quick to give Him the credit for your success. Your model of dependence on Him in an independent environment will lead your children to do the same. Stay relentlessly reliant on your Savior and Lord. Then wealth remains a blessing and not a burden. Use the world's wealth as leverage for other-worldly purposes. This is confirmation of a growing relationship with Jesus Christ. Therefore, grow wealth and give wealth for His glory!

God's Part

God delights in rewarding faithful managers of His wealth—both in this life and in the life to come.

My Part

_____

_____

_____

_____

_____

Everyone's Battle

"I do not understand what I do. For what I want to do I do not do,
but what I hate I do."
Romans 7:15

Everyone battles bad behavior. Becoming a Christian does not obliterate bad behavior. Becoming a Christian gives you the Spirit of Christ to choose good behavior. However, the battle still rages. We know the eternal war is won with our salvation in Christ, but the temporal battle with sin does not cease at salvation. You are naïve to think otherwise. It is spiritual warfare that requires spiritual weapons. Fighting behavioral battles in your own strength leads to defeat. Do not be cocky with your Christianity. It is not a safety net for bad choices. Rather, it is the power of God for wise decision making.

Still the battle over bad behavior is a daily engagement. You know you need to be patient, but you lose your temper instead. You know you need not covet another woman, but your lust lingers. You know you are to exercise forgiveness, but you harbor resentment. You practice peace "faking" when you should be humbly confronting. You lie when you know you should be honest and trust God with the outcome. Your pride and ego self-promotes, while you know in your heart you should give God and others the credit and the glory. These conflicting behaviors do not go away. You find yourself feeling defeated, because you once again gave in to behaving badly. How can this cycle cease? How can we prepare for this sly suicide bomber of bad behavior? This self-inflicted terrorism can drive you crazy. It can even lead you to give up on God. "After all," you say, "this is the guilt I gave up at salvation." The battle over behavior is wearisome, but do not give in or give up.

God cares. God understands. He is there with you moment by moment. In spite of behaving badly, you are not any less a Christian. And He does not love you any less. He feels for you in your conflicting emotions and actions. Most of the time He will not erase the negative consequences of your sin, but He will certainly stay with you during this eruptive time. God does not flee from your failures. He is there to help you pick up the pieces. He is there to help you learn from your mistakes. He equips and empowers you to win this particular behavioral battle in the future.

Do not be overwhelmed by the onslaught of the enemy on multiple fronts of your life. Fight each battle one at a time and watch God win. Seek out a

Dose 50

mentor to coach you into wise living. Learn how to depend on the Spirit of God living through you. His grace is sufficient. He who lives in you is greater than he who lives in the world. No behavior, no matter how bad, can separate you from the love of your heavenly Father. There is no condemnation in Christ Jesus. Start by being honest about the ugliness of sin that still seeks to influence your attitude and behavior. Become more self-aware of blind spots that cripple your relational effectiveness with others. Learn how to live by faith and not by sight. Seek reconciliation with another you may have offended or who may have offended you. Avoid magazines and Web sites that flame your lust.

These are everyone's battles, and these are battles that can be won. Fight with the weapons of God's wisdom and truth, and not man's ingenuity. Let Him fight on your behalf. Be accountable to God and man. Move beyond the guilt of failure to the non-condemnation in Christ. In Christ is everything we need to fight everyone's battle!

God's Part

God's love through Christ covers a multitude of sins, and He promises that with each temptation we face, He makes a way of escape.

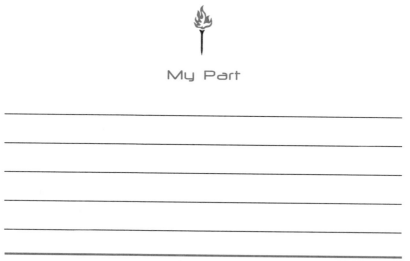

My Part

_____

_____

_____

_____

_____

Radical Restoration

*"Though you have made me see troubles, many and bitter, you will restore
my life again; from the depths of the earth you will again bring me up. You
will increase my honor and comfort me once again."*
Psalm 71:20-21

The need for restoration implies something has been lost or
taken away. The joy of your salvation is gone. It is in need of restoration. Your
passion for God has become apathetic. It is in need of restoration. Your marriage
has grown stale. It is in need of restoration. Your career path is at a dead end. It
needs restoration. Your life in general seems to be in a downward spiral. It
desperately needs restoring. The need is there and now is the time to begin the
restoration process.

Restore means to bring back into existence. An old dilapidated house can be
restored with fresh paint, wood and a lot of hard work. Antique furniture stored
in a dusty but dry barn can be brought out, cleaned up, stripped and restored to
its original look and design. Restoration is a beautiful process to watch. The old
passes away and new becomes front and center. It is a metamorphosis, a changing
of the guard. Objects are restored all the time, but few people take the time to
restore their life.

Just like a soiled piece of wood, the stain from your sin needs to be removed.
It may take some abrasion from God's heavenly sandpaper to remove its effect.
Your bad habits may cover your life like dust on an original oil painting. Begin
the process of letting God and others clean off the surface of your life and then
work their way down into the depths of heart change. Restoration can happen,
but it takes time. What took you years to "behave yourself into" will probably
not experience full restoration overnight. You need to stay committed to the
process and stay engaged with God, because He is the father of restoration. This
is His expertise, and His completed work is breathtaking. the restoring work that
God can do with a submitted life is truly amazing.

You have tasted the freedom of God's forgiveness. It is still there for the
taking. Do not let your shame keep you from asking for forgiveness. Restoration
begins by asking for forgiveness. This is foundational. Restoration is predicated
on honesty. You have to be honest with God, yourself and others about your
blind spots, bad habits and wrong perspectives. Honesty is the best attitude for
restoration. You have to understand where you are and what needs to happen to

Dose 51

move you forward. Restoration implies that it will not be pain free and it will cost you something. But it will be more than worth the effort. It may take gallons of stripper to clean away the mess in your life, but be patient. The beauty below the sin is what God has intended for you all along.

If you allow God to do His thorough work (which He does so well), there is a good chance you will receive more honor and comfort than you have ever experienced. A restored life is a broken life pieced back together by the grace of God. Your pride is weaker than before. Your faith is stronger than before. Your gratitude is much more abundant than before. Your expectations are based on God's character, not your selfish whims. This is the beauty of a divinely restored life. You are more appealing than the original. No longer is your faith tentative. By faith you now allow Christ to unleash Himself through your everyday living. People are in awe of God because of His beauty in your life. You are almost unrecognizable compared to the old you. In Christ all things have become new. God has restored you for His purposes!

God's Part

The God of creation is in the restoration (redeeming) business, revealing what He originally intended—something good.

My Part

_____

_____

_____

_____

_____

_____

Pay Attention

"The Lord will make you the head, not the tail. If you pay attention to the commands of the Lord your God that I give you this day and carefully follow them, you will always be at the top, never at the bottom."
Deuteronomy 28:13

Pay attention to God's voice and to His directives. His ways are the best ways. His ways are the wisest ways. Most of His commands are clear as a bell. You do not need a Greek lexicon to understand "love God" and "love people." His principles for living are for our good. Seeking godly counsel is for your good. Do not seek out advice from those who will tell you what you want to hear. Solicit wisdom from those who diligently apply God's Word to their daily life. You need those around you who will prescribe Scripture to your life. They may offer God's truth with tough love or tender care. Be extremely grateful for both. It is the truth of heaven that transcends your life and confirms your heart and mind into Christ-likeness.

Therefore, pay attention to what God is saying through others. You may not want to hear what they are saying, but still listen. Allow your anger to subside for a moment, so the Lord's way of doing things can give you much-needed perspective. The enemy is not your spouse, your child or yourself. You are not sleeping with the enemy, though the enemy does seek to dupe you into this delusion. The enemy is the master of deception, the devil himself. Therefore, fight for your family and not against them. Fight the enemies of anger, distrust, disrespect and lovelessness. Love does cover a multitude of sins. Apply it liberally and lavishly. Love unconditionally and others will respond accordingly. Pay attention to applying the love of Christ. As He loves in you and through you, you are capable to love others with the same passion and persistence.

Also, pay attention to God's work around you. Your circumstances are part of His greater canvas of creation. Your situation is part of God's plan to accomplish His larger purpose for your life. Do not get sucked into the short-term setbacks; instead, keep the fires of faith burning. This momentary affliction is for a season. You may be experiencing God's discipline to develop your own discipline.

Or, this pause may be needed to involve others whom God would have you to bless. See your current circumstances as part of God's bigger plan. Pay atten-

Dose 52

tion to where He has you. Do not become preoccupied with where you want to be. Be faithful today and tomorrow will take care of itself. It is all in God's timing. You can trust His timing. Indeed, pay attention to the little things. Be excellent around mundane and insignificant issues. Like carefully crafted bricks of a sidewalk lead to a large and inviting home, faithfulness in the little matters leads to larger opportunities. Moreover, pay attention to your soul. If it is sick and tired, allow God's love and grace to nurse it back to a robust and engaging condition.

Your life will be limited unless you pay attention to your soul care. This caps your capacity prematurely. An unkept soul is like an unkept engine—eventually the car quits running, and so shall your life. Solitude, planning, thinking, meditation, confession and repentance will do for your soul what a healthy diet, rest and exercise do for your body. Treat it well. Pay attention to what matters. God matters most. First pay attention to Him, and you will not lack passion paying attention to His prevailing priorities. Paying attention pays!

God's Part

God promises to promote the one who is faithful in the little things to oversee great things.

My Part

_____

_____

_____

_____

_____

Purposeful Promotion

*"For the Scripture says to Pharaoh: 'I raised you up for this very purpose,
that I might display my power in you and that my name might be
proclaimed in all the earth.'"*
Romans 9:17

God is a purposeful promoter. He promotes those who don't seem deserving, and He holds back those who seem deserving. Yet, His process serves His purpose. He takes lemons and makes lemonade. He takes a bad leader and accomplishes good results. Sometimes it doesn't make sense or even seem fair, but the perceived inequities are all a part of His plan. For example, if this one door of opportunity had not remained closed, you probably would have missed the current opportunity that better suits you. Now you are much better positioned to honor God. After all, God's purpose for your elevation in responsibility and recognition revolves around the display of His power. It is a little scary. Your role has changed and you feel a sense of inadequacy and your trust has become tenuous.

Do not let the trepidation found in your new surroundings cause you to be someone you are not. Be yourself—God has called you first and foremost to be you. You are to be you for Him. You will fail if you are not you. You are not like the last leader. You are not some phantom leader that projects a caricature of you. You are just who God wants for this assignment. You can rest in being you and trust that this is more than adequate. Yes, you will grow in character and leadership—no doubt. But, your leadership transformation will not compromise your God-given wiring and temperament. Those whom God raises up, He resources. He resources with relationships. He resources with wisdom. He resources with ability. Give Him recurring credit for your newfound opportunity. You are here to serve for a season. Execute His plan with grace and skill!

But what about those whom God promotes that are undeserving of this awesome responsibility? First, it is not for you or me to judge. How can we ultimately know what is best for the situation or for the organization? It is God's call. Therefore, if it is God's call, we can rest in His ability to make the right call. Left to us, we might default to what makes sense or to what is circumstantially expedient. God's purposes are much more eternal in scope and strategy. He can display His power in brilliant colors as easily through a hard heart as a tender heart. This doesn't always make sense, but it is true. It is counterintuitive, but it

Dose 53

is part of the genius of God. This is how the influence of God transcends govern-ments with unbelieving leaders. God's purpose will not be thwarted by man's pride and arrogance. In fact, many times it is enhanced. The contrast of world-views is so stark that counterfeit living is exposed with glaring flaws. What man messes up, God picks up, cleans up, and raises up.

Sometimes the enemy is allowed to have his way so that God can display a better way. He does work it out. Do not grow discouraged, be encouraged: There is a greater purpose at work. God may have you in the wings to step in and implement a turn around. When people, families or enterprises are down, the only way to go is up. Be patient. God is working. He will promote you in His timing, for His glory. Keep your jealousy of the undeserving one in check. Erase jealously with kindness, contentment and gratitude.

God's purposes are much larger than a person. He is working in spite of us or others. Regardless, point people to Jesus. He always satisfies!

God's Part

God promotes whomever He wishes, and He doesn't need people to second-guess Him.

My Part

_____

_____

_____

_____

_____

Child Discipline

*"Folly is bound up in the heart of a child, but the rod of discipline
will drive it far from him."*
Proverbs 22:15

Children need discipline and children desire discipline. There is
nothing more frustrating for a child than non-existent rules or for the rules to be
constantly changing. Having no rules is a challenge for a child because they lack
a context for wise decision making and understanding. Decisions need to be
black and white. When children understand and master the black-and-white
decisions, they can then graduate to the gray decision-making world of adults. It
is easy to understand first-time obedience. However, it is not always easy for the
child to remember to obey again or to follow through. Nor is it always easy for
the parent to enforce the rules. But this is the heart of discipline for a child and
for a parent.

The wise parent models instant obedience in their decision-making and in
their attitude toward authority. Children are smart. When they see automatic
obedience modeled by mom and dad, they are compelled to do the same. When
they see inconsistent obedience in their parents, they are repelled by its hypocrisy.
A child's obedience can be limited by the quality of the parent's obedience. If you
run a red light, you risk your child running right past your instructions. If it is
good enough for dad, it most certainly must be good enough for his child. If you
are too busy to pray, read the Bible and apply it, then when your child transitions
into puberty there is a good chance he or she will do the same. Children many
times follow your footsteps. Your discipline will have the moral authority
required as you model obedience to God, government, boards and bosses—even
the rules you dislike!

The effective discipline of your child takes time. There are no shortcuts.
However, your time investment and consistent discipline on the front end can
save you a ton of time, money and heartache on the back end. Children who are
lovingly disciplined tend to be teenagers who are teachable. Even the best of teens
still have their "moments," but in their heart of hearts they default back to the
discipline of their childhood. These God-given boundaries administered by their
parents are freeing for children. They are freed from unhealthy relationships, and
they are freed from the guilt of sin. Their decision-making is not perfect, but it is
positioned in a God-fearing framework. Strive for grace-based discipline with

---

Dose 54

your child. Avoid anger and harshness. Match the punishment with the severity of the offense. Save your severe "bullets" for the really blatant sins like disrespect, dishonesty or disobedience. Do not shoot a "flea" with a "cannon." Children push back from parents who overreact.

Vary your discipline. One child requires a spanking while the loss of a privilege is more effective for your less-compliant one. Discipline needs to be adapted to various ages and circumstances. Remember, the overall goal is to instill instant obedience. It is helping your child understand the consequences of a wise decision versus a foolish decision. Delayed discipline will come back to haunt you. Be engaging. You cannot delegate discipline to church or school. Parents, pray for your children; work together by supporting each other's decisions. Talk in private over differences of how to discipline.

A disciplined child has a much better chance of becoming a disciplined parent, who lovingly disciplines his or her own children. Therefore, dare to discipline for your grandchildren's sake!

God's Part

Our loving heavenly Father disciplines us as His children, and He provides wise instruction on how we should model and give discipline to our children.

My Part

_____

_____

_____

_____

_____

Rest Secure

"Let the beloved of the Lord rest secure in him, for he shields him all day long, and the one the Lord loves rests between his shoulders."
Deuteronomy 33:12

You can rest secure in Christ. He is your security system for living. Nothing will infiltrate His care without His warning light of love being set off. He loves you so much that He provides the security of Savior Jesus. He saves you from yourself. He saves you from hell. He saves you from sin. And, He saves you from insecure living. You do not have to be insecure. You are secure in the Lord. You can rest securely in this.

Insecurity will "eat your lunch." Insecurity haunts your head. It is a barrage of bad thinking that slowly and most assuredly deteriorates your faith. Insecurity is to faith what water is to fire. It douses the flames of your faithfulness. Your trust in God teeters in the face of insecurity. Insecurity is food for fear. You feel like you don't measure up as a husband, wife, parent, friend or employee. Your mind begins to play tricks on you. You feel anxious and ineffective. This is the fruit of insecure living.

However, there is no need for the follower of Jesus to be intimidated by insecurity. Insecurity is insidious and unfair. It will keep you from commitment. It will block you from the bountiful love of God. Loose living is rooted in insecurity. It unleashes you from the mores of God's principles. A life of insecurity will come unbundled when it is blindsided by life. Adversity can be an anvil of pain. Pain promotes insecurity. You can hide your insecurities until you are squeezed. Pressure reveals your true self. However, you do not have to RSVP to insecurity's invitation. You can shun its influence and succumb to your Savior instead. It is in the Lord that you can rest secure.

God is there to strap you on His back if necessary. Like a wounded soldier on the battlefield of life, you need the medic of heaven to nurture you back to health. Do not act like you have not been wounded. Your soul has been lacerated by lack of love. Your heart is hemorrhaging because of the crushing effect of rejection. Fear has inflicted a head wound of disillusionment. Now is the time to lay your insecurities at the feet of Jesus. You are secure in Him. He binds up the brokenhearted. He is salve for your wounded soul. Jesus is security in an insecure world. He is a rock of security in the ever-shifting sands of life's transition. He is

Dose 55

calm in a world full of calamity. He is peace in the face of fear. He is courage in uncertain circumstances. Therefore, rest in the security of the Lord. Cease from striving to change things that are out of your control. Trust His tender touch. Hold His hand. Follow His secure path and you will learn to rest in Him. Because you are His beloved, you are dearly and deeply loved by Him. It is His sincere heart of love that holds you secure. Rest secure in the reality that you are a cared for child of King Jesus. He has your back. And sometimes He carries you on His back. It is a secure place to be.

In Christ you are shielded from insecurity. Yes, there may be remnants of insecurity that seek attention, but in the Lord their voices remain weak and inaudible. Walk away from the insecurities of your past. It is only a seductive shell of fear. Instead, bask in the warm canopy of God's security. His secure love is your escort. Nothing can separate you from the love of God. He is your life. He is your motivation for living. His ways are your blueprint for life. Secure your security in Christ. You can rest secure in Him!

God's Part

God's commitment to His children is an eternal, now and forever, commitment. He promises never to leave nor forsake His own: That's true security!

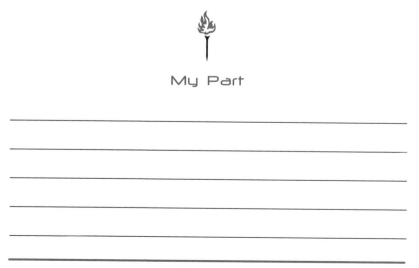

My Part

_____

_____

_____

_____

_____

Disputable Matters

*"Accept him whose faith is weak, without passing judgment
on disputable matters."*
Romans 14:1

Disputable matters are differences of opinion over what
is acceptable to God and not acceptable to God. These are really gray areas that
we are tempted to use as a club of conviction on another believer in Christ. The
purpose of disputable matters is not to get us worked up over another's perceived
"sin." So relax. The purpose of disputable matters is to trust God with His judgment over the issue and to accept the person with whom there are conflicting
standards.

Satan would rather us "major on the minors" and miss the significance of
people dying without Christ in their hearts and food in their stomachs. The
enemy's goal is to suck us into the sideways energy of debating issues that pale in
importance over exercising patience, joy and generosity. In the big scheme of
things, what is really important to God? That's where He invites us to put our
focus and passion. You may be a better debater and a more mature Christian.
You can quote Scripture with the best of them and make a very compelling argument for your point. But, if you alienate and crush your weaker brother (not
your opponent), what has really been gained? Do not use your liberty as leverage
to look down on another. Nor are you allowed to use your legalistic standards to
hold others hostage on behalf of your behavior. We are all on a pilgrimage of
understanding and maturity. Rather, accept one another and trust God with any
judgment that may need to occur. To usurp His authority is to play God. This is
not a fun game to play, and someone eventually gets hurt.

The mature one in the faith knows better. The initiative to reach out and
accept starts with the mature. Ask God for wisdom and grace to coach another
when asked, and to mentor by your life's example. Your life lived in the power of
the Holy Spirit is the best teacher and exhibit of Jesus. When disputable matters
arise, keep the focus on Christ. What would Jesus do? How would Jesus act? You
can't improve on Jesus. He hung out with sinners. He turned water into wine.
He accepted and forgave prostitutes, adulterers and dishonest businessmen. He
abhorred religious pride and hypocrisy. Those with teachable hearts He loaded
down with truth. To those with unteachable hearts He told stories. Therefore, for
Jesus' sake, replace a condescending attitude toward the weak in faith with one of

Dose 56

compassion. Be challenged and convicted by their zeal to obey God. On the contrary, you may struggle with seeing others taking too much license with the grace of God. Do not let your disagreement with their behavior keep you from learning from them. Ask God to grow you and change you in areas where you may be too inflexible or unrealistic. It is OK, even preferred, for you to fear God and love God at the same time.

Moreover, disputable matters need not drive us apart, but they can bring us together. If we were both the same, then one of us would be unnecessary. Allow Christ to keep your motive clean. Do all things for the benefit of another, placing their well-being before yours. You can be right in the letter of the law and lose the spirit of your influence. Or, you can accept, not judge, and not only keep a friend but extend your influence. Let your gracious attitude override the temptation to drive home a point. The Holy Spirit will work way beyond your capabilities. Disputable matters can become a catalyst for Christ-likeness with all of us!

God's Part

The Lord is displeased with those who cause a weaker brother to stumble; He is gracious and patient with all and expects mature believers to behave likewise.

My Part

_____

_____

_____

_____

_____

_____

Model Mentoring

"Even when I am old and gray, do not forsake me, O God, till I declare your power to the next generation, your might to all who are to come."
Psalm 71:18

Your life is a stewardship. Owned by God, He expects us to invest in others. This is who we are as followers of Christ. Part of our life management is giving back to younger men and women in the form of mentoring. We mentor others because someone took the time to mentor us. Or, we may mentor others because we did not have a mentor and, as a consequence, we stumbled and bumbled around until we found our way. The opportunity for mentoring compels us to protect others from our own mistakes. God can use our life experiences to help young men and women not to repeat bad history and to create good history. This is an important process of wisdom transference from one generation to the next. More important than the transfer of wealth is the transfer of wisdom.

Wealth without wisdom can lead to wickedness or, at the very least, weirdness. And we do not need to set up others for either. In fact, in some ways it is easier to pass on wealth than it is to pass on wisdom. The transfer of wisdom takes time and understanding. It takes getting involved in someone's life to the point that it costs you something. More than likely it will cost you time, money and relational equity—your most valued assets.

However, by investing in someone through a mentoring relationship, think of the savings. You may save them from the heartache of a messed-up marriage. You may save them from the gut-wrenching experience of not getting to know their children. You may save them from a stupid business decision that leads to insolvency. You may save them from chronic indecision and insecurity because their identity resides somewhere else other than in Christ. Your mentoring is a cost-saving proposition. Everyone wins in the mentoring process, especially the mentor!

However, gray hair does not automatically qualify you as a mentor. Your first qualification as a mentor is an unyielding submission to your heavenly Father. Because of your love and fear of God, He is your model for mentoring. You are patient when you need to be patient. You confront when you need to confront. And, you ask tons of caring questions. Mentoring is not revealing all of the

Dose 57

answers. Rather it is helping another through the process of discovery. Yes, there are times to give ardent direction and warnings, but many times it is sharing what you have learned and are learning. It is asking the one being mentored to take your life experiences and God-given wisdom and, prayerfully, apply it to their own life. Your goal is not a clone of yourself (God help us). Your goal is a passionate follower of Jesus Christ.

A wise mentor will transfer humility, gratitude, teachableness, contentment, selflessness, forgiveness, discipline and grace. It is a character-driven model. Mentoring without character is like driving a car without gas. It is not possible. Hold high a standard of living life on purpose with a bent toward God, and then invite others to join you. The masses will not flock to be mentored, but a few will. Go with a few and watch God do a work of wisdom that eventually influences the masses. Model mentoring, for it makes men and women!

God's Part

God owns us and invests experience and wisdom in us. He then grants us opportunities to invest in others.

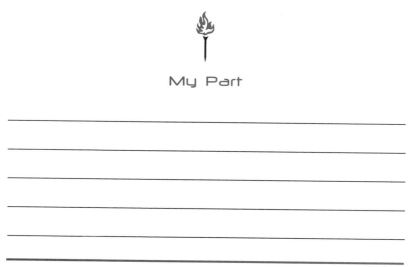

My Part

_____

_____

_____

_____

_____

Stand Up

"The Lord said to Joshua, 'Stand up! What are you doing
down on your face?'"
Joshua 7:10

There is a time to pray, and there is a time to act.
There is a time to listen, and then there is a time to do. There is a time to weigh
your options, and there is a time to choose what's best at the time. Prayer gives
you clarity on what needs to be done, and faith gives you courage to follow
through.

If you know what to do but are still praying about it, you are praying extra,
useless prayers. There is no need to delay your decision anymore. Do not hide
behind the need for prayer. God's Spirit has made clear to you next steps. Now is
the time to act. It may be confronting a friend over their path of destruction. It
may be resigning from your job. It may be breaking off a relationship. It may be
a short-term mission trip overseas. It may be a phone call, an e-mail or an in-
person visit seeking forgiveness. Whatever God has already told you to do, do it
quickly. There is no need to delay the inevitable. You are better off dealing with
this sticky issue sooner than later. If you wait any longer, you will allow anger to
permeate your thinking.

Obsession with someone or something other than Christ will distract you
from God's best. Now is the time to stand up and move forward in the power of
the Holy Spirit. Push fear aside. You cannot control the response of the other
person or the fallout from the confrontation. But, you can rest in the fact that
the Lord is leading you through this process. As you communicate, He will give
you the words to say, in the right spirit. Yes, there are times it is easier to pray
than to act, but prayer without action is presumption on God. So get up from
your passive posture, and translate your prayers into gracious and passionate
obedience.

Standing up does require faith. The level of faith that brought you to this
point will not "cut it" going forward. Faith needs are fluid. For this next stage of
living you will need a larger beaker of belief. Leverage off your faith that led you
to Christ, but do not stay there. Stand up and move forward in the power of the
Holy Spirit. God has prepared the way. Set fear aside. Place it back in the closet
of intimidation and shut the door. God has great things in store for you, but it

Dose 58

requires greater faith to stand up and move forward. Yes, there are unknowns that sometimes haunt you, but this is when God shines the brightest. It is on the cloudy course of uncertainty that God's Word illuminates your path. Read, believe and act on His Word. This is your assurance. Remaining where you are is not an option. We are either growing by faith in Christ, or we are regressing in fear. There is no middle ground. If you stay put in passivity, you will digress in discouragement. Your step of faith may be the very thing needed for others to do the same. Your life is a catalyst for Christ-centered living.

Yes, there is a battle to be waged, and sometimes the enemy infiltrates into your own relational ranks. Do not underestimate his influence. He may even use his "Christianity" as a badge of deception. Do not be intimidated by his lies. Stand up to "sin in the camp" with truth. The truth of God cannot be bought or used for selfish purposes. Rather, it is a cleansing agent for individuals and communities. Speak the truth in love and watch God work. His truth cuts to the chase. It dives deep into the heart of the matter.

Stand up in love, empowered by the Holy Spirit, with the Word of God on your breath. This is faith in action. Since you have prayed, now you can act!

God's Part

God delights to stand beside the one who stands—and acts—in obedient faith.

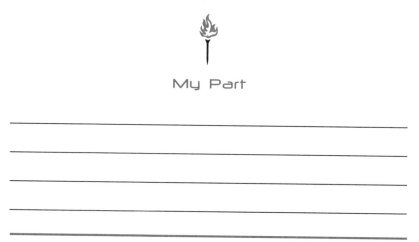

My Part

_____

_____

_____

_____

Bad Examples

*"Now these things occurred as examples to keep us from
setting our hearts on evil things as they did."*
1 Corinthians 10:6

Bad examples can be effective teachers. You may have been exposed to poor parenting as a child. Let this be a lesson on how not to parent. Do not default to the bad habits of your mom and dad. They did what they could, but now you know better. Do not stay mad at them for their poor example. Rather, learn from them. Display the opposite of their attitudes and behaviors that were counterproductive and relationally destructive.

Your supervisor at work may not be the best in the world. In fact, he may be a jerk. Humility and patience are the only things keeping you from lowering yourself to his volatile temper and demanding spirit. One day you will be the boss, and because you have been a victim of the wrath of an insecure leader, you will not do the same. You do not wish their dysfunctional management on another. You are learning from this leader, who is a bad example. Do not stay angry with them, but thank God instead, that by His grace you will not be the same. Instead, you will be a loving and loyal leader.

Or, maybe your lessons from a bad example stem from a friend or colleague. You have witnessed the pain and the sad consequences of their poor choices. Their example of bad decision making is loud and clear. Their impulsiveness and inability to receive advice is literally destroying everything and everyone around them. Others have chosen to worship the gods of this world. Sexual immorality, money, ingratitude and busyness have all eroded their ability to enjoy God, enjoy people and enjoy life. You can learn from their mistakes. Use this time to take notes of what not to do. Whatever someone of ill repute does, simply do the opposite. Over time your good example will shine as a light of hope to those who walk in the darkness of their bad example.

There may come a time when you seem to be the only hope for those who have stumbled around in their bad choices. Be there for them. Your current ability to refrain from caustic criticism will earn you the right to help them when they finally turn from living badly. You are no better than them, just better off. Do not let your good example in many areas go to your head. It is only by the grace of God that you are not a poster child for behaving badly. Your good exam-

Dose 59

ple is an asset that God has blessed you with, and as such it is not to be taken for granted. Also, do not let your good standing become a pulpit to preach down to those who are poor examples. Your life already speaks louder than your words. In a good way you are providing hope for those around that seem hopeless.

Bad examples do not need a lecture over the plight of their errors. They already feel the hollowness of self-absorbed living. What they need is someone who will accept them but not their lifestyle. Bad examples are really searching for good examples. You have been blessed with the moral authority to help. Bad examples need help badly. Do not do what they do or say. Do the opposite. Learn from their failures and mistakes. Be there for them as a good example. Bad examples can be good teachers. Therefore, go to school and learn from them!

God's Part

God holds up poor examples for us to learn from and, if possible, to minister to.

My Part

_____

_____

_____

_____

_____

Character & Competence

"And David shepherded them with integrity of heart;
with skillful hands he led them."
Psalm 78:72

Authentic leadership is a mixture of character and competence. You cannot have one without the other and provide healthy leadership. Competence without character is like a magnificent ivory-white ship's sail that lies collapsed without wind. Character without competence is like a strong gust of wind without a billowy sail to capture its effect. Both are required for the level of leadership that God expects. Character is the linchpin of leadership. It is truly the measure of a man. Your character is your union card: It earns you the right to participate in leadership. Your depth of character determines your breadth of leadership. Character is forged on the anvil of life's experience. When your obedience to God intersects with life, character is developed. It is through a relationship with Christ and a relationship with people that you understand and develop character. God's Word defines character, and living life is your opportunity to apply character. You can choose to be a character, or you can seek to live a life of character. God's will is the latter. People want leaders that are dependable. Someone they can trust. They want leaders that are available to listen and understand. A leader of character follows through on commitments and does what is right even when it costs him personally. You can have average skill with exceptional character and still be an extraordinary leader. This is how God works. He works from the inside out. Sometimes your great abilities get in the way of a definitive work of character in your life. Anything you have is because of the grace of God, so thank Him for your abilities and allow Him to mold His character into your life.

Competence on the other hand gives you a platform to exercise your character. You are gifted and skilled a certain way. It is imperative that you understand how you are wired. This self-awareness is your ticket to improvement. What you know today is not sufficient for what you need to know tomorrow. This is why competent leaders are ever learning. Current circumstances and future opportunities beg for your education. Skilled leaders ask lots of questions of those who have walked before them. They research and read about other successful leadership and organizational models. This is part of sharpening your skills. A stagnant leader is an unattractive leader. Focus on your sweet spot. Spend your time on

Dose 60

the number one thing you do best. If it is recruiting, then recruit. If it is raising money, then raise money. If it is coaching, then coach. If it is crunching numbers, then crunch numbers. If it is managing a home, then manage a home. But, in the process become the best at what you do and who you are. Yesterday's competency will not stand against today's needs. Passion does not equal expertise. Just because you want to do something does not mean you need to do it. Make sure that your skill set and experience matches your "want to." Otherwise, you are setting yourself and others up for frustration. My passion will not improve my golf game unless I am skilled with hand-and-eye coordination. You can be sincere in your endeavors and still be involved in the wrong situation. Make sure you live and lead in environments that nurture and grow your giftedness. This type of leadership development molds you into a leader worth following. Your competence gives you credibility, while your character sustains your credibility. Apply both, and then watch God work. Character with competence is your ticket to authentic leadership. Let these two be your guide, and God will use you beyond your own capabilities. Lead on!

God's Part

God gifts each of us with strengths in certain areas, and He provides the tools and mentors we need to develop them. He also creates situations designed to grow our character so that, with both character and competency, we can serve Him and others.

My Part

_____

_____

_____

_____

_____

Expanded Vision

"When Joshua was old and well advanced in years, the Lord said to him, 'You
are very old, and there are still very large areas of land to be taken over.'"
Joshua 13:1

Increased age need not limit your vision. Instead, your advancement in years can be the very time to expand your vision. Now is the time to leverage your experience, your resources and your relationships for a larger vision. Your slowing down can contribute to the speeding up of the vision. Your role is to let go and allow God to accelerate His greater purpose. This makes sense. You have planted, others have watered and the next stage of vision development is God's great increase. His Kingdom economy is poised for a major expansion, and you get to facilitate this portion of His vision. It may be the training of leaders, the writing of books, the deployment of funding or the mentoring of men and women.

Do not let your "winding down" let down the vision of God. You are uniquely positioned for this stage of life, to prepare for the expansion of God's vision. Your influence is compounding, not waning. Now is the time to become laser beam focused by pouring into a few leaders with your time and resources. Select faithful friends who are aligned with your same God-sized vision. Place on them the mantel of your mentorship, and free them to move forward in the power of the Holy Spirit.

The world puts out to pasture the aged. However, followers of Christ lift up and honor the wise, worn and weary warriors of the faith. Partner with a protégé who can prolong the passion of your life. This is God's plan. He does not waste a lifetime of faithfulness. On the contrary, a faithful life is fertile soil in which to launch an even greater vision on behalf of the Kingdom. Your greatest influence is yet to come. Indeed, the faithful dead sometimes speak louder than when they were alive.

So, pray for God to raise up a faithful few who in turn will train others. Look for men and women who have a track record of obedience to God and a hunger for Him. Your life is an epistle. Open it fully and without reserve, so these eager and energized hearts can read it with great humility and learning. Your failures could become their greatest ally, as they learn from your mistakes. They will commit their own "crimes" of Christ-less living, but hopefully not yours.

"He who walks with the wise grows wise, but a companion of fools suffers harm." Proverbs 13:20

Dose 61

Moreover, there is a word for the passionate protégés. Honor your maturing mentor with time and teachability. Your way may not be the best way. Listen intently to what God is saying through His faithful servant. You may be limiting God's vision. Do not undersell the Spirit of God. His heart is the world. He is the God of the nations. God's vision is global. Think in terms of international implications. This is the make up of heaven. It is a multicultural mantra and mandate that He has for you. There is an expanded and God-sized vision that needs to lead and motivate you. Stay broken and prayerful before your heavenly Father, and He will entrust this to you.

Hold everything with an open hand. It is imperative that you learn much now, so that you can lead most effectively later. Pour the footings of His vision's foundation deep and wide. Then experience God, as He builds His expanded vision. A God-sized vision is the fruit of multiple lifetimes. It is multigenerational. His vision is an eternal expansion. Therefore, do your part with excellence and trust Him with the heavenly results of His part!

God's Part

God so loved the world that He gave. And, He expands the vision of His people to share that love with the world in new and exciting ways.

My Part

_____

_____

_____

_____

Good Examples

"Follow my example, as I follow the example of Christ."
1 Corinthians 11:1

Good examples are rare but rewarding. Some are hard to find because they are discreet and busy about doing the right things. Though good examples are few and far between, they can be found. They can be found in matriarchs and patriarchs. They can be found in new believers and old believers. They can be found at work, on the golf course, in the boardroom, at a Bible study or in church. Good examples can be found, but it is important that you pray and go to school on them. Pray to God for good examples to cross your path; then you will have the privilege of watching them "up close and personal" or from a distance. Regardless of their proximity, it is wise to learn from their lives.

You can learn a ton just by looking. Look for how they invest their time and money. Look for the way they love God and respect their spouse. Look for their intentionality in loving non-Christians. Be a character watcher. Watch their patience and forgiveness in the middle of a firestorm of criticism and adversity. Watch for the confession of their sin and shortcomings with a heart toward repentance. Watch them fear God and serve people. As you watch, there is a good chance you will become like them. You are tremendously influenced by what you watch. Watch good examples. Moreover, read their writings. Understand their thinking and question their habits. Find out what they do and why they do it.

Once you discover their "best practices" for living, begin to incorporate them into your life. Of course, integrate these disciplines only as you are ready and it is appropriate. Be yourself, while you learn from someone else. You are still sold out to Christ first, and only follow the good example of one who follows Him. You are not in a fan club for man. Instead, you have a lifetime membership in Christ's Kingdom.

Jesus is your best example. However, relating to Jesus is sometimes hard, because He was without sin. Yet, He is the standard. If you are in doubt about a behavior or attitude, emulate Jesus. Jesus will never let you down or lead you astray. The saintly characters of the Bible are good examples to follow as well. Abraham's faith is compelling. The boldness of Moses gives courage. Joseph's integrity is inviting. His forgiveness is refreshing. David's brokenness is pure and

Dose 62

holds eternal consequences. Esther's loyalty is inspiring. Solomon's wisdom is life changing. Hannah's trust is without compromise. Jonah's zeal is challenging. Elijah's dependence on God is a faith builder. Job's perseverance is rewarding. Jeremiah's compassion is humbling. Isaiah's eloquence is heavenly. The Minor Prophets reveal a major need to fear God. The Psalms of David comfort. Jesus is Jesus. Paul perseveres. Peter preaches. Luke writes. John loves. Zacchaeus reaches out to sinners. Mark didn't give up. These are good examples. Indeed, there are other modern-day good examples. There is Billy Graham's integrity, Mother Teresa's service to the poorest of the poor and John Paul's leadership.

Be inspired by good examples. Be encouraged by good examples. Be taught by good examples. Be motivated by good examples. Be set free by good examples. Be a good example. But, make Jesus your best example!

God's Part

Although all people have "feet of clay," to the degree that God is at work in and shines through their lives, to that degree they should be emulated.

My Part

_____

_____

_____

_____

_____

Child Training

*"Train a child in the way he should go, and when he is old
he will not turn from it."*
Proverbs 22:6

Child discipline and child training are similar, but different. They are similar because the desired outcome for both is a child with a heart for God and love for people. The end goal for each is a Christlike character. But there are some real differences between the discipline and training of your child. Discipline is more reactive; training is proactive. Discipline many times is a consequence of negative behavior, while training seeks to develop positive behavior. Training educates the child on the "why" behind the "what." Discipline is more concerned with the "what." Training is motivated by teaching the child "how to fish," not just "giving them a fish." Discipline in some ways is easier and takes less time. Training is more involved and takes hands-on effort from both parents. Discipline is focused more on the short term, while training looks toward the long term. They both overlap and both are vital to the healthy upbringing of your child.

Ultimately, you are training your child to be a responsible and God-fearing adult. Think of the training as on-the-job. You can tell your child to do something, and they may forget. You can show them how to do it, and they will probably remember. However, when they experience it for themselves in hands-on fashion, there is a much better chance of follow through. This is at the heart of training. You help your child experience life under your apprenticeship. You are there to teach them, encourage them and mentor them. Yes, they will fail along the way, but you will be there to help pick them up. It takes parental wisdom, because you do not want to rescue them prematurely either. God may be in the process of teaching them a valuable lesson.

Take driving an automobile, for instance. This is freedom for the teenager and fear for the parents. The grown-up child can finally spread his wings in two tons of steel going 55 miles per hour. His peripheral vision is blurred and it's hard for him to remember the speed limit. In the meantime, the parents' prayer life is escalating to new levels of intensity along with the price of their insurance premiums. Learning to drive a car can be a great training time. This can become quality time for the dad and the child. Yes, have the teenager take a defensive driving class, but it is just as important to have them take a daddy driving class.

Dose 63

Buy them a mechanically sound, used "practice car." Instruct them in the basics of proper yielding and how much a speeding ticket costs. Let them experience the responsibility of paying for the insurance. This is great training in the realities of life.

Lastly, train them to "stand alone." Standing alone means they have the confidence in themselves and the trust in God to do the right thing even when their friends don't. Give them leadership responsibilities around the home like chores, care for animals and planning trips. Teach them how to think. Let the Word of God be their training manual. Reward them for applying its principles. Help them discover their passion and what they do best. Encourage them to follow God's calling, even when it makes you uncomfortable. Take the time to train your child today and they will be trained for a lifetime. Train well!

God's Part

God has provided us His training manual: His Word! He leads and guides His children with hands-on experience, expecting us to do the same.

My Part

_____

_____

_____

_____

_____

_____

Passive Husband

*"So Ahab went home, sullen and angry because Naboth the Jezreelite
had said, 'I will not give you the inheritance of my fathers.' He lay on his bed
sulking and refused to eat."*
1 Kings 21:4

A passive husband is a poor leader. He lacks leadership for his
wife, his children and his work. His passivity may be a result of many things. He
may be stuck in neutral because he feels overwhelmed. The thought of doing
anything locks him down. He may be unable to function as a leader because he
didn't get his way. If he can't do things his way, he will not do them at all.

He may be passive because his dad was passive. This is the only role model
he has ever known. A man may be suffering from chronic passivity because his
confidence has been crushed. He has never recovered from a traumatic event that
sent him into a sequence of bad choices. Or, a man's lack of action may be a
combination of these or other reasons. He is like a turtle perpetually stuck in his
shell, afraid to come out and face the realities of life. He may be going through
the motions of life, but something is missing. The fire to engage life has been
extinguished, or is only flickering at best.

If that describes you, it is time that you awoke from your slumber of irre-
sponsibility. Your wife and others have covered for you long enough. You are on
the verge of losing what you have worked for all these years. More importantly,
the respect of your wife may be quickly vanishing, and your credibility in the
community may be eroding. Now is the time to take the reigns of your responsibility and do something. Lead, follow, or get out of the way. Eventually, however,
you need to lead. This is your role and calling from God as a husband, a father
and a man. Leaders are made, not born. Indeed, this is probably a huge faith
issue for you. Nevertheless, these are opportune times to model, for those who
love you, explicit trust in God.

He understands your apprehensions about leadership. Your heavenly Father
is your leader. You can lead, because He leads you. Lead as He leads you. Model
His leadership. You cannot improve on the leadership style of Jesus. Because He
leads you as a servant, you can lead as a servant. Because He leads you with
humility, you can lead with humility. Because He leads you in love, you can lead
in love. Because He leads you with patience, you can lead with patience. Because
He leads you with compassion, you can lead with compassion. Because He leads

Dose 64

you with purpose, you can lead with purpose. Because He leads you with courage, you can lead with courage. Because Jesus led, dependent on His heavenly Father, you can lead dependent on your heavenly Father. The Holy Spirit is the leader of your life. Submit to His leadership—He will move you from passive to active leadership: a leader led by the Holy Spirit. When you are led by God's spirit, you will lead. It is as natural as falling off a log.

Yes, you will fail along the way. But it is better to fail as a Spirit-led leader than to do nothing in your own strength. This requires faith, especially for a husband to take a risk as a leader. Faith overcomes fear and failure. Your leadership at times will let down your wife, but she will love you even more as she experiences your leading in love. Giving her everything she wants is not leadership. Giving her a husband led by the Holy Spirit is what she needs. Trust God to take care of her wants. You give her what she needs. A passive husband sucks life from relationships. An engaging husband gives life to relationships. Be a life-giver by trusting God with your leadership. Lead for God's sake!

God's Part

True to His promise, Jesus did not leave His followers alone. He sent His Spirit to lead, guide, encourage and empower—making simple men the kind of leaders who turned their world upside down!

My Part

_____

_____

_____

_____

_____

Grace Works

"But by the grace of God I am what I am, and his grace to me was not without effect. No, I worked harder than all of them—yet not I, but the grace of God that was with me."
1 Corinthians 15:10

Anything good in your life is a result of God's grace. Your success is the result of the grace of God. Your money, your possessions, your spouse, your children, your job and your relationships are all a result of God's grace. You cannot take credit. Yes, you have been available and obedient, but only because of the grace of God. He is the originator and sustainer of all good things in your life. If you ever hold on to anything with a tight fist or take credit for His "grace work," then you are in danger of losing His blessing.

Acknowledge regularly who is responsible for the pleasant and productive things in your life. If you struggle with your lot in life, still be grateful for the grace of God that is at work in you. Your personality, your looks and the way you make a living are all a result of God's grace. Your health, your opportunities, your goals, your aspirations and your dreams are all grace driven. His grace is there for your recognition, reward and results. Celebrate His grace. Embrace His grace. Revel in His grace. His grace is infinite in supply and available, "real time." Be careful not to take His grace for granted. Grace taken for granted may cease to be granted. Credit grace for its great effect in your life.

Without the grace of God, we maintain at best and are miserable at worst. Without the grace of God, we grope in the darkness of indecision and run out of steam. Without the grace of God, we are lost in our sins and servants of Satan. Without the grace of God, our heavenly rewards are meaningless and lacking. The grace of God is the glue that holds life together. It is the fuel that energizes your life. Without a doubt, grace is what God is about. It works.

The grace of God works hard. There is no conflict between grace and work. They go together. It is because of God's grace that you work hard. Your good works are a result of grace. Grace is not a result of your works, and grace without works is dead. This is why grace work has the most impact for God's Kingdom. Grace work transcends human effort. Your efforts are limited without the grace of God. The grace of God can accomplish twice as much through you in half the time. This is the pattern of grace work. You work hard; you work smart; but you

Dose 65

work motivated and inspired by God's grace. How do you know you are engaging in grace work and not just good work? The object of your affection is an evidence of grace work. Grace work dies daily to self and lives for Christ. In celebration of its accomplishments, grace work points to God and others. Grace work is also grateful. There is a sense of deep appreciation and gratitude for those empowered by the grace of God.

And, lastly, grace work is quietly, humbly and relentlessly on point to carry out the will of God. There is no opposition or discouragement that derails grace work. Focus wins the day every time! Invite the grace of God into your work. Acknowledge God's grace in your work. Most importantly, depend on the grace of God in your work. Grace work works smart and hard. It is Kingdom motivated and Kingdom productive. You are who you are by the grace of God. You work hard and are refreshed by God's grace. Therefore, grace works!

God's Part

No one deserves the grace of God, it is His free gift.

My Part

_____

_____

_____

_____

_____

Revival of Joy

"Will you not revive us again, that your people may rejoice in you?"
Psalm 85:6

Life can squeeze out your joy. Like an exhausted slice of lime or lemon, there is nothing left. You have flavored the life of others by giving to them, but now nothing remains for you. Your joy is gone. You need a revival of joy. Maybe you are battling health issues or financial woes. The pressure has gotten the best of you. Like the crushing of grapes in the preparation of wine, your juices of joy have been depleted. The only remains are dried and parched skins. You are tapped out. You are in desperate need of a jolt of joy. You need joy to bridge you from your position of burnout back to your role as joy giver.

Isn't it ironic that we can fall victim to the very thing we see as a deficiency in others? No one is immune to slipping into a joyless life. In fact there will be seasons that joy will elude us like water in the desert. We need a new infusion of joy. The revival of joy is ongoing. You can only run so long, and then you must stop and refill your joy tanks. You can remember when work brought you joy, but now you are maintaining at best. Marriage was bliss in the past—full of joy—but now you just coexist. Your relationship with God once erupted with joy, but now it is stale and distant. A revival of joy refills you on all these fronts. Revival assumes that joy once existed. Joy reigned over many aspects of your life, but certainly the joy of your salvation was once preeminent. To revive something means you bring it back into existence, back to life. So the best place to start the revival of anything is God.

God specializes in resurrecting and reviving. He can take what is dead or dormant and breathe life into it. The breath of God gives joy. God's breath is not stale or repugnant. On the contrary, His breath is fresh and rejuvenating. Like an asthmatic gasping for air, we struggle in need of God's oxygen. Life's struggles wear us down to a pulp. We need the breath of God to revive our joy. But, you may need to alter your proximity to benefit from the breath of God. His breath is most effective up close and personal. Like an inhaler, you need God daily in your face to transmit His joy.

The joy of the Lord is not captured from a distance. It is inhaled and ingested from a position of intimacy. Do not let your joylessness leave you incoherent. God wants to clear your heart and mind. Joy is on the way, like the arriving of

Dose 66

the cavalry in the heat of the battle. Let God rescue you, revive you, and set you back on a joy-filled journey. You are not defeated in Christ. The enemy is the loser. He is the joy killer, but his advances are temporary. Allow God to resuscitate your joy. The world won't. Work can't. People fail. And money is an illusion of joy.

So go to the creator, dispenser and sustainer of joy. Lean on the one full of joy, Jesus. He will bring your joy back to life as He was brought back to life—full and robust. Let Him make your joy complete. His joy is your strength. Some things never change and His joy is one of them. Start by simply thinking back on when you exchanged self for a savior. You opened the door to your life and Jesus entered with a housewarming gift. It was a beautiful basket full of joy. Relive that experience and reengage with Him. His joy is not jaded—it is just right. Your joy will rub off on others, and the revival of rejoicing in God will extend from one person to another. Be joyful in Jesus!

God's Part

God specializes in breathing new life into those who need it most—us!

My Part

_____

_____

_____

_____

_____

Business Alliance

"So give orders that the cedars of Lebanon be cut for me. My men will work with yours, and I will pay you for your men whatever wages you set. You know that we have no one so skilled in felling timber as the Sidonians."
1 Kings 5:6

There are times your business or ministry requires expert attention outside of your skill set. You can attempt to save a buck and improvise yourself, or you can trust someone much more competent to carry out the task. A wise man is one who sticks to only what he does well. Otherwise, he becomes a "jack of all trades" and a "master of none." Stick to what you do best, and outsource to others who are the experts. It may cost you more in the beginning, but in the long run it will not only save you time—it will make you money. This is harder for a resourceful, frugal, "pull yourself up by your bootstraps" kind of entrepreneur. However, many times this is God's best plan. He doesn't expect you to have all the resources and gifts to carry out all that needs to be done. On the contrary, He knows you need help.

Nonetheless, let's look at your need for resources outside of your scope of capacity. Why create a department or division within your enterprise that does not reflect your core competency? Instead, seek out and interview other companies that can do this extremely important task more efficiently and more effectively, without causing your organization to convulse over change and a redirection of capital resources. Wise is the leader who understands his limitations. Stay focused on what you do the very best, and others will come to you as experts in their field. Experts are experts because they focus on one area of expertise.

Your business alliance may be with believers or unbelievers. This is part of your role of being "salt and light" to the community. When you have to engage with the business world, you make a statement. Hopefully, it is a statement of integrity and honesty. Simply by doing what you say you'll do, others will take notice. Make it your number one goal to utilize people of character, who execute their work with excellence. The "gravy" will be if they are Christians. Sometimes the "Christian" label gets in the way of the deliverables.

So, be wary of individuals or organizations who wrap themselves in the flag of their faith. Let their work do their talking. If they can prove themselves to be effective in one short-term project, then they can be trusted with a more long-

Dose 67

term and capital-intensive relationship. In working relationships, always date before you marry, or you may be begging for an annulment. Get to know someone for at least a year before you engage in any kind of significant project. Why jeopardize your resources and reputation by letting emotions get in the way? Stay disciplined to the process and accountable to the people. Gather around you an advisory board to help you navigate these business alliances. One nugget of wisdom may save you a year of sideways energy within your enterprise.

In a word, we all need experts whom we can trust to compliment our core competencies. Seek out these individuals or companies and engage them at the appropriate time with your trust and with your resources. A focused leader with an open hand is poised for growth and opportunity. Be the best at what you do and trust others to do the same!

God's Part

God gives certain skills to one person and other skills to another, because in His economy there is strength in unified diversity.

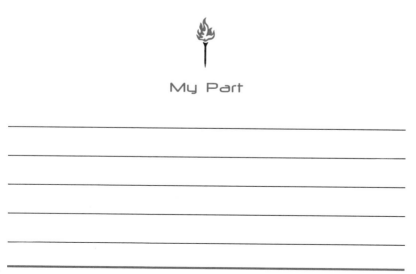

My Part

_____

_____

_____

_____

_____

Thanksgiving to God

"You will be made rich in every way so you can be generous on every occasion, and through us your generosity will result in thanksgiving to God...
Thanks be to God for his indescribable gift!"
2 Corinthians 9:11, 15

Gratitude to God is a natural overflow of generosity. The gift of His salvation in Christ is indescribable! He gave when we did not deserve. He still gives, even though we are undeserving. His gift of liberty is freeing. His gift of health is healing. His gift of relationships is rich. His gift of peace is calming. His gift of wisdom is confidence. His gift of the Holy Spirit is comforting. His gift of finances is security. His gift of Himself is reassuring and humbling.

Gratitude explodes from our hearts when we are reminded of His generous gifts. They are incomparable and incomprehensible! Thanksgiving to God is a tremendous opportunity to unleash joy. This is one of the fruits of gratitude. We have "Joy, joy, joy, joy down in our hearts," because He came down to earth and into our hearts. This is an occasion for a righteous, even raucous, celebration. Gratitude to God can be a moment-by-moment expression. Even in the middle of the worst of circumstances, your thanksgiving to God is appropriate and needed. Look beyond your current condition to your heavenly hope. He has prepared a place for you, and His preparations are not shabby! They are just what you need and desire.

So, your thanksgiving is for what He has done in the past, His current provision and what He has prepared for you in the future! God's generosity is without competition. His liberality in giving wins out every time. You can be very, very grateful for this. Let thanksgiving escape from your lips often. Use it to put out the fires of fear and worry before they spread too far. Thanks be to God, for you are made rich!

Yes, in Christ you are made rich. You have everything needed for this life in Christ. As a consequence of your management of His riches, you can be ridiculously generous. This is the natural result of thanksgiving. Because of your deep gratitude to God, you are called and compelled to give. Gratitude invites you to generosity. You cannot experience authentic thanksgiving and not see it birth giving. It is a beautiful process. Because God has given to you, you give to others. At the moment you receive the gift of God, generosity is conceived in your heart.

Dose 68

This is why your heart feels pregnant with thanksgiving. It will explode without the regular birthing of generosity to others. This expression of gratitude results in action. It is tangibly and regularly giving to people for whom Christ died. The poor need food, a job and Jesus. Orphans need parents, a home and Jesus. Divorcees need acceptance, healing and Jesus. The angry ones need gentleness and Jesus. The confused need clarity and Jesus. The bankrupt need financial wholeness and Jesus.

The opportunities abound that invite your generous expression of gratitude. Gratitude is one of God's prescriptions for discontentment. The two cannot comfortably coexist. Thanksgiving keeps the credit for your accomplishments on God and others. Without either you would not be in your current position of influence and success. Gratitude is generous. Gratitude is content. Thanks be to God for His indescribable gift!

God's Part

God makes His children rich in every way so that they can be generous in every way.

My Part

_____

_____

_____

_____

_____

Time Management

"Teach us to number our days aright, that we may gain a heart of wisdom."
Psalm 90:12

Time can manage you or you can manage time. Time can be allusive or it can be a servant to God's will for your life. Time management begins with teachability. It is the admission that you need to learn how to better manage your time. If you do not manage your time well, chances are that you do not manage your life well. Your life has become a series of reactions rather than one of intentionality.

Of course there is no way to perfectly plan your day or your life. God is the one in control. But, He expects us to steward the time He has given us in a profitable fashion. Time management is not unlike budgeting money. There is a limited amount and it needs to be handled wisely. There is a financial plan for giving, investing and spending. So it is with your time. Your volunteer work is your giving back to the community. It is your service in the church. This is your giving of time in its purest form.

Then there is your investment in people. Mentoring, coaching, counseling and simply being a friend are common ways to invest in others. The most valuable investment is in those who do not know Christ. Your temporal time investment in unbelievers will leverage throughout eternity as they come to know Jesus. And, lastly, consider the wise spending of your time. This is your day in and day out usage: Phone calls, meetings, e-mails, meals and planning are all part of your time spent. Make sure this is not a mindless routine. There should be alignment of your activities with your God-given purpose in life. If not, you may need to change your work environment or how you spend your free time. Time is your most valuable asset, so manage it well and it will seem like you have more. This is God's way of redeeming the time!

Time management is learned. Let God be your teacher. He created time, so He understands its intricacies. Time is finite, but its applications are infinite. Indeed, He will help you allocate and prioritize its use. It is the wise use of time that creates more capacity and minimizes frustration. God will instruct you if you ask Him. He will dispense His wisdom to all who will take the time to listen. His wisdom will reveal your limitations, because you cannot and should not do everything. We all need the help of God and others. The wisdom of God will

Dose 69

lead you back to trust. It is a trust issue. God can be trusted to provide just the right amount of time to accomplish His will. Since this is the case, you can implement the most important activities and trust Him with the things that do not seem to get done. Do you have a hard deadline to leave work by six in the evening? When this self-imposed deadline rolls around, trust God with what is not yet done and go home to your family. This is priority living based on faith in God.

Every stage of life has its own priorities, so let God's Word and others help you define your priorities. And allow room for interruptions. It is naïve to think that your time allocations will work flawlessly each day. Life happens. People need things that are not on the day's or meeting's agenda. Allow for breaks between appointments, because inevitably people run late or meetings run over. Best of all, hire someone gifted in managing your schedule and trust, train and empower them to execute. In the middle of your busy and productive life keep an eternal perspective or your life results won't matter anyway. A wise heart treats each day as a gift from God, with the attitude that it could be the last. So live each day by faith in the one who is the timekeeper. Take the time to manage your time!

God's Part

God is the inventor and keeper of time; He best knows how to manage and prioritize everything under time's domain.

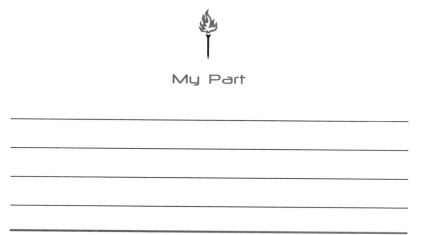

My Part

_____

_____

_____

_____

_____

Wise Process

"Then the king said, 'Bring me a sword.' So they brought a sword for the king.
He gave an order: 'Cut the living child in two and give half to one
and half to the other.'"
1 Kings 3:24-25

A wise process protects. It protects life. It protects relationships. It protects resources. It protects commitments. The process on the surface may not seem smart, but time wins you over with its wisdom. Indeed, it is tempting to bypass the process. After all, you know what needs to be done, or so you think. It is tempting to barrel ahead into activity because the need is so great and the time seems so short. Nonetheless, even if you are confident of the needed outcome, still trust the process.

At the very least it will involve others who need the process to gain understanding of the requirements and support for a new role. For example your work may require a new position to be filled. Will you fill this role with the first interested warm body, or will there be a defined process for the protection of the company and the protection of the one being interviewed? The rule of three is normally a wise process to employ. Interview three legitimate and good candidates with the purpose of selecting one. During the process of interviewing you may discover new issues related to what the job really requires. You may even rewrite the job description. Moreover, this process of employee selection needs to invite four or five other interviewers. Their perspective and wisdom is invaluable as you seek to discern the most qualified person for the position. "People processes" need not to be rushed so that everyone is protected from unwise decision making. Opportunity evokes emotion. Process channels it into better options.

Jesus understood this. He spent a 30-year process of preparation before He embarked on a relatively short three years of ministry. In addition, He took His followers through a process of discipleship, teaching and on-the-job training. His process with people was pregnant with questions, discovery and hands-on experiences. Ultimately, His process culminated with the cross and the resurrection. Therefore, some processes require death before there can be life. The death of a vision may be needed before it can be realized.

Hence, we are all in a process. We are all learning along the way in preparation for God's next assignment. Process grooms you for greatness. If you run ahead of the process, you may very well disqualify yourself from greatness.

"He who walks with the wise grows wise, but a companion of fools suffers harm." Proverbs 13:20

Dose 70

Therefore, it is wise to be patient in the process and enjoy its excursions. Your vision may be dormant at best, or even dead for now. Do not give up on its feasibility. This may be part of God's bigger process. Process is His protection for your family. Without a prayerful process you might overcommit—to the neglect of those who need you the most. Indeed, you can implement prayer immediately as your number one process component. Make Christ your process consultant. Default to "what does Jesus think" before you ask Him to bless your "seat of the pants" process. Prayer is your best process. Employ it well and employ it often. Allow prayer to define the process, initiate the process and conclude the process. Prayer that seeks the wisdom of God and the wisdom of godly counselors is almost guaranteed to be a great process.

Therefore, weave prayer throughout the process and watch God work. Allow the Holy Spirit to drive the process. Hearts, minds and spirits align around a prayerful process. You can't beat a process permeated with intercession and punctuated by prayer!

God's Part

In the fullness of time, God sent the Savior—He had a process to complete… not a minute too soon, not a minute too late.

My Part

_____

_____

_____

_____

_____

Captive Thoughts

"We demolish arguments and every pretension that sets itself up against the knowledge of God, and we take captive every thought to make it obedient to Christ."
2 Corinthians 10:5

Thoughts need to be taken into captivity. They are dangerous left alone to their own devices. Untamed thoughts can be alluring and illusive at the same time. They can lead you down the path of lies and destruction, or they can lead you into the open fields of truth and life. Left unattended and without boundaries, thoughts can become reckless and harmful. You become what you think, not unlike your body becomes what you eat.

There is a direct correlation to thinking and doing. Sloppy thinking leads to sloppy living. Disciplined thinking leads to disciplined living. The mind can be a beautiful agent of the Lord or a seductive siren of Satan. It is the beautiful mind of Christ that you seek above all else. But this will only happen with intentionality. Your mind must first pass through the "boot camp" of obedience. This is basic training in thinking. The purpose of your thinking is obedience to Christ. If this outcome is not clear, then you are set up for failure. Obedience to God is the bottom line of Christian living. Without obedience to God, we have no authority or credibility. Hence, our understanding and application of truth becomes tainted and watered down.

Obedience gives you the momentum to confront the enemies of truth. Indeed, atheistic and agnostic arguments will assault and challenge your Christ-centered beliefs. Your biblical worldview will collide with worldviews diametrically opposed to grace and forgiveness. Your belief in absolutes will be ridiculed and roasted over the fires of relativism and humanism. Therefore, prepare your mind by understanding the nuances of your faith. Why do you believe what you believe? How is Christianity relevant? What historical facts point to the resurrection of Christ?

But captive thinking is more than an apologetic of the Christian faith. Captive thinking is pure thinking. Obedience to Christ can be expressed in an unadulterated commitment to Him. A pure mind is compelled by an intimate relationship with Jesus. He is the groom and we are the bride. The bride is enamored and in love with her new husband. She is captivated by her man. She wants to please and serve him like no other. It is a love relationship that won't quit! It's

Dose 71

the same as we fall deeper in love with Jesus. We want to think what He thinks, do what He does, go where He goes, listen to what He listens to and watch what He watches. Your eyes are the sentries to your mind. They stand on guard ready to act in a moment's notice. Do not overwhelm your eyes with the self-inflicted wounds of lust and licentiousness. It is hard enough for them to guard your mind without your capitulation to sin's exposure. The Devil's demons sit on your shoulder feeding you bad information, but they are powerless. They cannot make you do anything. The demons can speak lies, but they are impotent in their ability to make you behave badly. Learn to recognize the origin of these twisted thoughts, and then quarantine them into God's hand. Thus, you give the captured thoughts of the enemy to God. God can handle these prisoners of pain.

In contrast, release the captured thoughts of truth and purity into your life. Wise and pure thoughts lead to wise and pure living. As a result, your obedience to Christ is alive and well. Sometimes taking thoughts captive is like herding cats, but stay on point. Do not drop your guard or relax your efforts. Your "Waterloo" is your mind. Stay vigilant to bring each thought into captivity. This is battle one!

God's Part

The Lord provides limitless "good and perfect" things for us to think upon: the beauty of Himself, His creation and His Word.

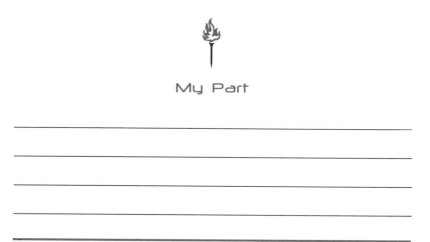

My Part

_____

_____

_____

_____

_____

Effective Accountability

"As iron sharpens iron, so one man sharpens another."
Proverbs 27:17

Accountability is essential for the follower of Jesus Christ. We are accountable to God and man. Accountability comes in many forms, but the results are the same. The outcomes of accountability are integrity to our commitments and follow through in God's will for our lives. We all do better when others are watching. The details of your life may be blurry to most. But, when you surround yourself with trusted advisers, by faith you give them the reading glasses to your heart and soul. They see and understand your motives—the good and the bad reasons why you do what you do. Unencumbered, you share with them your struggles, sins, and fears.

Accountability is a safe and trusting environment. Through it you slow down and take the time to allow the hard questions—questions that deal with your time in God's Word, your thought life, your financial health, your marriage, your work, and your time, to name a few. Nothing is off limits or sacred to the truly accountable. Accountability is most effective when you sincerely submit to others. It's no good if you limit your accountability to individual silos, because you can hide behind these linear relationships. It is when you invite collaboration and a small group perspective that you open yourself up to a 360-degree evaluation. It is easier to fool the one than the whole.

Find a small group of four or five with whom you can grow old together—people who can smell you blowing smoke miles away when it is only a small cloud on the horizon. They can read you because they really know you. They know your tendency to drink too much, to blow up in a fit of rage, or to take your wife for granted. They know how your unguarded strength can become your greatest weakness. They help you to keep these pitfalls in check, but they also affirm your progress and success. Accountability is as much a positive reinforcement as it is a negative warning or rebuke. Ultimately, true accountability partners point you to God.

God is the standard. His Word holds the rules of the game. When an issue is under debate, biblical principles veto anything that smells of foolishness. Submission and obedience to God is the foundation and the goal of accountability. He is still there when no one is watching. He understands the motives of our

Dose 72

hearts when we ourselves are confused. Fear of God is good and effective accountability. What you say and do does matter. It matters for today and it matters for eternity. Your respect and love for God becomes so strong that you want to do His will no matter what. Your desire to grow in His character is what drives your life. This type of God-conscious living grows your accountability over time. You discover God's expectations on your life that you never knew existed. And, you become freed up to know that in some areas you have imposed limits on your life that God never intended. You have limited yourself with self-imposed restraints that are not a part of God's accountability.

Effective accountability with God requires time and transparency. Seek His face and ask what needs to change in your life. Let others know what God is teaching you and ask for their mutual accountability. Submit to God, caring friends and your spouse. Accountability leads to freedom. Be set free!

God's Part

God is the ultimate accountability partner, but He has also given us brothers and sisters in Christ—including our spouse—to help keep us on track.

My Part

_____

_____

_____

_____

_____

Battle Fatigue

"David went down with his men to fight against the Philistines, and he became exhausted....But Abishai son of Zeruiah came to David's rescue; he struck the Philistine down and killed him."
2 Samuel 21:15b, 17a

"Doing life" is a heavy battle to endure. There are days the fatigue of your faith is at a breaking point. You grow weary of financial struggles. The pain of separation has sapped every ounce of energy from your being. The pressures at work have crushed your spirit. It seems like one additional problem could send you over the edge. You may be suffering from spiritual battle fatigue. This is the time to regroup and engage in the encouragement of other Jesus followers.

Spiritual battle fatigue is the time you are the most susceptible to sin. Now is not the time to add another initiative, or you could flail away, faithless and vulnerable to unwise decision making. Indeed, there are friends in your life whom you can trust for counsel and direction. It is imperative for you to get under their accountability. Accountability is something given by you. So, use this time of exposure to submit to their support and good advice. If you plow ahead, however, you are taking unnecessary chances. Exhaustion blurs the mind and deceives the heart. When you are spent is not the time to confront conflict. A tired life faces conflict at a disadvantage. Either you lash out in anger over the injustice you are feeling, or you lose your patience and judge others prematurely.

Do not be embarrassed to admit that you need a break. This is a time to explicitly trust others for a season and not to teeter on the edge of exhaustion. People are waiting in the wings to rescue you. Yes, it is humbling to think we need to be rescued. But without the assistance of a friend or relative, you may very well collapse under the weight of the burden you are bearing. Confess your need and accept their help. Everyone will be blessed as a consequence.

Battle fatigue also requires reengagement with God. Your sweet time with Jesus is required to gain back your strength in Him. Your inner resolve is renewed by focused time with your heavenly Father. He understands the demands of your world. He is there to renew your mind with the truth of His Word. He is sensitive to your damaged heart, and with His comfort and love He will extract the fiery darts of the enemy and bring healing. He recognizes your frail faith and is positioned to inject it with hope and peace. God specializes in "soul care" by

"He who walks with the wise grows wise, but a companion of fools suffers harm." Proverbs 13:20

Dose 73

giving rest and refuge to exhausted lives. Moreover, while God is strengthening you, Jesus is fighting for you. He is the righteous warrior par excellence! The battle scars of Christ were born out of heated moments of engagement with Satan himself. Jesus understands the wiles of the devil. He has met him face to face and has overcome Him by the Word of God. And so shall you. Indeed, you have the privilege of submitting to the Lordship of Jesus so that He can fight for you. In your own strength, especially in your place of exhaustion and fading faith, you are no match for the unseen enemy. He will use mind game tactics and emotional sabotage to get you to give up on God. Now is the time to call upon the name of the Lord. He will save you from yourself. He will save you from Satan. He will save you from sinners. He will save you from success. He will save you from exhaustion.

God is your righteous rescuer, who is poised to invade the enemy's territory. Do not be shy to invite Him into the battle with you. Your faith may be waning, but men of flesh and blood are not the foe. Spiritual battles require spiritual resources. Therefore, seek His face and apply His resources well!

God's Part

God gives grace to the humble (those who admit their need).

My Part

_____

_____

_____

_____

_____

Patient Perseverance

*"Let us not become weary in doing good, for at the proper time we will reap
a harvest if we do not give up."*
Galatians 6:9

Patient perseverance is required to see the fruit of your labors. It
takes time to penetrate hard hearts and to influence those outside the faith.
Family members can be especially difficult to love. This is why you have the
family of God to serve and love. Sometimes you feel closer to your family in
Christ than you do your biological family. This can even be discouraging, but do
not take it that way. Rather, accept the fact than blind people grope in the darkness and need special attention. They are very limited and may be incapable of
giving any direction or unselfish leadership. This is the nature of their condition.

You will be continually disappointed if you expect non-Christian family
members to bend toward your interests and desires. For instance, you have an
event that means the world to you, such as the graduation, birthday or marriage
of a child. Do not expect an unbelieving relative to care. They are self-centered
by nature. This is how they live life every day. It is a chore and a burden for them
to give. They are oblivious to the need for celebration of this momentous occasion for you and your loved ones. Indeed, they are rejecting you by their absence.
But you can let go of this hurt. Like a helium-filled balloon, release it to heaven.
Let go of this offense and give it to your heavenly Father, who certainly understands. Non-Christians act like non-Christians. So do not be surprised. But you
know better—you will continue to do good because it is the right thing to do. You
will reap a harvest, though the reward of its fruit may be stored in heaven!

So, you still serve even when you are not served. You still love even when
you are not loved. You still forgive even when you are not forgiven. You still celebrate important occasions even when your important occasions are ignored. You
still listen even when you are not listened to. You still care even when you are not
cared for. This can take its toll in wearisome service and giving. But do not give
up—the Word of God will make a difference. Your life is making a difference.
God is using you in ways that you currently cannot comprehend.

Others are watching your unselfish acts of kindness. Your children especially
are watching. They are defining patient perseverance by the number one influencer in their life. Stay in the giving process for their sakes. Stay in the game for

Dose 74

God's sake. Ultimately it is all about Him. You remain unselfish for Him. You stay others-centered for Him. You give because Christ gave. You forgive because Christ forgave. It is all about being a good citizen in His Kingdom. Patient perseverance has nothing to do with demanding your way in your kingdom. Moreover, as you stay the course in good deeds, it leads others to Christ. This is the end game. This is the purpose for patient perseverance, so that others will see your good works and glorify God in heaven. You will probably be taken advantage of, yet it's all for the praise of our Lord.

Patient perseverance is for people and God. Do not give up on them. His timing is perfect. There will be a harvest and, for eternity, you will enjoy its fruit. Therefore, stay engaged in patient perseverance. Do not grow weary by depending on and looking to Him!

God's Part

God is the one who causes increase, both in physical fruit and in spiritual rewards.

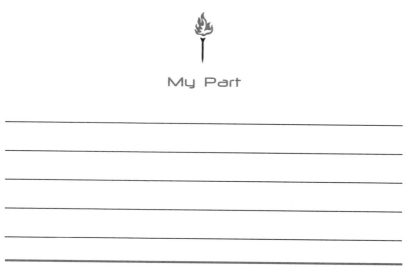

My Part

_____

_____

_____

_____

_____

_____

Mentor Mentors

"He made him master of his household, ruler over all he possessed, to instruct his princes as he pleased and teach his elders wisdom."
Psalm 105:21-22

Some are ready to mentor mentors. It is a little scary and you never feel totally qualified, but it is the right thing to do. The timing is right to go for it. You are a leader of leaders. You are a man's man. You are a woman's woman. It is time that you became very selective of those into whom you pour your life. You choose to mentor mentors because you know they are serious about developing others into passionate followers of Jesus Christ. These are men and women who serve their families, who build leaders at work and who press hard after God.

They already mentor. You are not trying to get them to mentor; instead, you are affirming them and providing them with mentoring resources. Even mentors need encouraging and a fresh perspective. Mentors are on the front lines getting shot up. They need another respected leader to assure them it is worth it. They need someone to help bind up their wounds, decorate them with a medal of courage, and commission them back into battle. No mentor can survive alone. They need the community of other like-minded mentors. They need someone to look up to, someone they respect and can learn from. Learning is the essence of mentoring. One truth you pass on to budding mentors is the valuable lesson of selectivity. Young mentors need to avoid time wasters. If a man is not faithful in his commitments, do not use God's good time to chase him down. There are too many others who value time with a mentor. Help these "wet behind the ear" mentors to hold those in whom they invest to criteria of high standards. Faithfulness is in the vortex of that qualification, because without faithfulness they will grow frustrated to the point of giving up. Give them the freedom—even encourage them—to walk away from the unfaithful.

Time is very precious and life is too short, so it is imperative to spend our time reproducing other mentors. Pray for people who will carry the mentoring torch long after you are gone. Look for people who are already influencers in their circle of relationships. These may be people who are mentoring and are not even aware of their influence. In some ways these oblivious mentors are the best kind to be mentored. They are naturally gifted by God for this role. People automatically go to them for counsel and advice. They already serve as a personal

Dose 75

coach for others. Your role as a mentor of mentors is to affirm their current role as an informal mentor and to provide them with a little more structure. Help them balance spontaneity with structure. Indeed, both are critical to the mentoring process. Another good relational investment in mentors can be found in a retreat environment. Go away for a night or two and allow participants to discuss what is and what is not working in their current mentoring situations. Keep it to a small group of no more that ten so that you can begin building a community of mentors. Retreats provide laser-beam focus on learning and encouraging.

Lastly, and most importantly, mentors need spiritual discipline. Help them to understand and to follow the ways of God. The wisdom of God goes a long way in equipping mentors. To the degree you stay fresh and hungry for God, your mentors will stay fresh and hungry for God. Discuss the Word together, memorize the Word together and apply the Word together. Submit to your younger mentor's accountability and ask them to do the same. Mentor mentors, because they need it. Mentor mentors, because you need it. Mentor mentors for the sake of future mentors. Mentor mentors, and watch God multiply your influence exponentially for His glory!

God's Part

Jesus promised to be with His followers in the disciple-making process (see Matthew 28), and responding to His call to mentor mentors is essential for true multiplication.

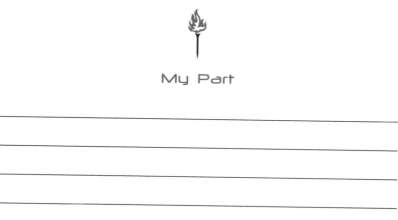

My Part

_____

_____

_____

_____

Extend Kindness

"'Don't be afraid,' David said to him, 'for I will surely show you kindness for the sake of your father Jonathan. I will restore to you all the land that belonged to your grandfather Saul, and you will always eat at my table.'"
2 Samuel 9:7

Kindness is a "killer application" for the Christian. It is "killer" in the good sense of the word. Kindness kills fear and replaces it with hope. It kills insecurity and replaces it with security. It kills rejection and replaces it with acceptance. It kills pride and replaces it with humility. Kindness kills the bad so that the good can have room to grow. Like the effect of a powerful herbicide on unwanted weeds, kindness cuts to the root of sin and infects it with grace and love. Indeed, the kindness you extend to others springs from a variety of motivations.

As a follower of Jesus, what compels you the most is the gargantuan kindness that He has bestowed on you. Undeserving, you were captured by the kindness of God. He captured your mind and in the process flooded it with kind thoughts toward others, even your adversaries. He captured your mouth and filled it with kind words of affirmation and encouragement, extending to those thirsting for verbal kindness. He captured your behavior and converted it to be others centered, so now you are guilty of random acts of kindness. Everything about you has the potential to exude kindness, because God is and has been kind to you. You can count on the kindness of God leading you and others to repentance. Kill others with kindness, and watch God bring them alive. It is the uncanny and counterintuitive nature of kindness. We have the capacity to be kind, because we have received His mercy as a "gift in kind."

Gratitude to God for His kindness is a sterling reason for us to extend kindness to others. However, gratitude also results from our horizontal relationships. You feel compelled to be kind to a family member or a friend, because of the kindness they extended to your child or your spouse. You can't help it. Kindness and gratitude are first cousins. When you are grateful, you search for ways to extend kindness to people. It may be a graduation gift, your presence at a wedding, or a handwritten thank-you note. You want to support those who support you and those whom you love.

Kindness has this powerful effect on people: It makes them care. It is the gift that keeps on giving. It seems you cannot pay forward enough with kindness. No

Dose 76

one has ever complained of receiving too much kindness. You cannot overdose anyone on kindness. On the contrary, it is healing and wholesome. Kindness is a picture of Christ. It is not only godly, it is God-like. Therefore, diffuse the rumblings of harsh words and replace them with kind ones. Otherwise, you can say the right words in an unkind way and defeat your purpose of being open and honest. People cannot hear what you say if how you say it is unkind. A kind delivery of hard words has a much higher probability of acceptance.

Kindness comes from a grateful and prayerful heart that is focused on Christ. You cannot help but be kind when you are captured by divine kindness. Extend the quality of kindness which has been extended to you. For Christ's sake, we can be kind to one another. The kindness of God invites an extended stay. This is the kind of kindness we all desire and deserve in Him.

God's Part

The kindness of God is meant to capture people body, soul, and mind. It leads a sinner to repent, and it causes the repentant one to extend the same kindness to others that he himself has received.

My Part

_____

_____

_____

_____

_____

Spiritual Leader

"For the husband is the head of the wife as Christ is the head of the church,
his body, of which he is the Savior."
Ephesians 5:23

Spiritual leadership in the home means that the husband serves. He serves his wife and he serves his children. This is not an option. This is who he is and what he does. Servanthood is at the heart of spiritual leadership. It is at the heart because this is how Jesus related to the church. He gave Himself up for the church. He sacrificed and served the church. It was not always easy and, ultimately, it led to the giving of His life. If a husband ever doubted his role, he need not look any further than Jesus. He is our role model of unselfish service.

So, your posture as spiritual leader in the home is not a power play. It is not a platform from which you whip everyone into shape. Rather it is an altar to God on which you to offer your ego and pride. There is no room for those twins of self-centeredness. Spiritual leadership replaces pride and ego with grace and humility. A spiritual leader is energized and empowered by the Holy Spirit. It is not about who wins or who is right. It is all about dying to self and serving your wife and children. Your service to them earns you the respect to lead them. If you default to barking out orders from your high horse, they may comply for a season; but you can count on them rebelling if there is no relational investment on your part.

Rules void of relationship do facilitate rebellion, or they may cause the family to shrink back into their corner of compliance, nursing a wounded heart. Indeed, most husbands do not feel qualified to be the spiritual leader. God knows that, and this is why He placed you in this role of responsibility—so that you can depend on Him. Pray to God and ask Him for His wisdom and grace to carry out your calling as spiritual leader. Seek out a mentor who can come along side you and give encouragement and coaching.

The easy way out is to ignore your responsibility by placing it on the petite shoulders of your wife. She may be more spiritually mature and qualified for spiritual leadership, but this is not her role. She is to follow your leadership. The wise wife will celebrate this and let her husband lead. This is how you both grow. Submission and servant leadership are excellent lessons of maturity in Christ. Let your husband fail. Love him enough to respect his spiritual leadership. Respect is

Dose 77

treating people at the point of their potential. A wife has the opportunity to see her husband for what he can become, not for where he is currently. Pray for him to pray with you and the children. Pray for him to read the Bible at the dinner table. Pray for him to be honest and wise about finances, both personally and professionally. Pray for him to be authentic about his struggles. Pray for him to know God. Pray for him to take the family to church. Pray for him to discover his spiritual gifts and to serve out of his giftedness.

Spiritual leadership takes a ton of prayer from the wife and the husband. A home led by a man who is a submitted servant leader is a home with a spiritual leader. Lead out of your weakness, and everyone becomes strong in Christ!

God's Part

God designed the home, and He ordains the roles within the home that work best and glorify Him the most.

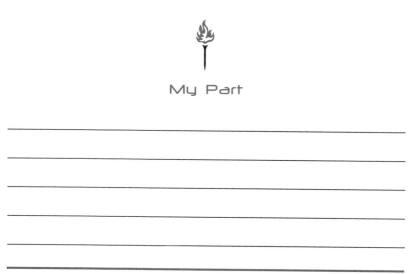

My Part

_____

_____

_____

_____

_____

Presumptive Praying

"But they soon forgot what he had done and did not wait for his counsel. In the desert they gave in to their craving; in the wasteland they put God to the test. So he gave them what they asked for, but sent a wasting disease upon them."
Psalm 106:13-15

Be careful what you pray for: You may receive it and more. And, it may not be pleasant! Prayer is not a magic wand that necessarily makes all things better. God is not a genie who resides in a magic lamp waiting for your beckoning call. He is not released by the "rub" of our prayers to grant our wishes. But, sometimes we drift into this presumptive way of thinking. We begin to take God for granted. And when things do not go to our liking, we ask God to bail us out or to act prematurely on our behalf. We sometimes act like spoiled children and demand our way. "OK," the wise parent may say to the child, "you can have it your way and its consequences."

Whether we are a child or an adult, we struggle with some of the same temptations. It may be an unwise purchase that sends our budget into chaos. It may be a relationship that chews up and spits out our emotional life. It can be a consuming career that has nothing left over for family or friends. It may be a hobby or a habit that has no Kingdom purpose. In fact, it devalues it. Somehow the issue comes back to control—my control.

However, since God can handle any situation, why do I try to force the issue? Part of the answer is fatigue. When I am emotionally, physically or spiritually spent, I do not make the best decisions. I ask for what I should not ask for. I do what I should not do. My praying becomes presumptive rather than prayerful. Presumptive prayers want a quick fix and a quick out. You are duped into thinking that God owes you this opportunity or relief. If you are persistent in your self-preserving attitude of praying, you may get it. But, your will is a cheap substitute for His.

Prayerful praying, on the other hand, is Christ-centered and patient. Through it you do really trust for God's will, not yours, to be done. It is a reassuring way to pray. The weight of the world does not rest on your way of doing things. God can and will handle things in His timing. You shift from a demanding spirit to a dependent spirit. You truly trust that God has your best interests in mind. He does not need to be conjured or convinced. Prayer is for us to align

Dose 78

our hearts with God's heart, not His with ours (that is a scary thought). Prayerful praying means you are searching the Scriptures to review good examples of prayer. You learn. Then your prayers grow in accuracy and authenticity. Prayer is an awesome responsibility not to be taken lightly or flippantly.

God delights in answering prayers that align with His character and purposes. This is who He is. This is what He does. Be prayerful. Be others-centered in your praying. Seek His face first, not His hand. Pray from a pure heart and a humble head. Prayerful praying beats presumptive praying every time. It is the way to go. It works. So be careful what you pray for. You may get it and more.

God's Part

As a loving Father, God understands what is best for His children and, sometimes, that means giving a willful child what he craves in order to teach him a valuable lesson: God's way is always best.

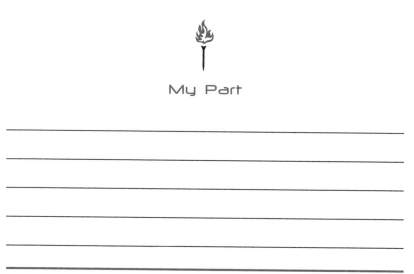

My Part

_____

_____

_____

_____

_____

Fear's Silence

"Ish-Bosheth did not dare to say another word to Abner,
because he was afraid of him."
2 Samuel 3:11

Most people do not speak in the face of fear. This is unfortunate for the leader who strikes fear into the heart of those around him. Fear is a cowardly caricature for motivating others. It may work for a short time, but it will come back to roost as a disloyal and demoralized team. Politics and backstabbing run rampant in fear-filled cultures. Wise leaders do not want followers silenced by fear. Rather, they need those who will speak their minds. Silent people provide no value to the enterprise. They serve only as humanoids in servitude to the system. This silent treatment is detrimental to the organization.

A healthy team is one that is not only allowed, but is encouraged, to challenge the system. A process that remains unchallenged will petrify into an ineffective routine of activity. This is one of the fruits of fear. If people are forced to embrace the status quo, then they feel backed into the corner of a fearful state, void of options. This is a poor position for productivity. Fearful followers become frozen into incompetence. They are afraid to change for fear of management's retaliation. This leadership by intimidation is lethal. Ironically, it eventually makes for lazy and lethargic team members. Fearful followers eventually lose steam and do just enough to get by. Fear-based leadership dislodges loyalty and replaces it with legalism. Who desires to follow someone because they have to? A much more noble motivation to follow is because people have the freedom to express their concerns and thus become a part of the solution. Wise is the leader who replaces his or her fear-based tactics with a conciliatory spirit, wrapped around collaboration.

Moreover, fear-based leaders are afraid themselves. They are afraid that their weaknesses will be found out. Paradoxically, they try to hide what everyone already knows. What a waste of time! Your weaknesses are already as clear as the color of your eyes to everyone. Thus, wise leaders will confess their weaknesses and learn to laugh at themselves. By stating the obvious, you are freed from the clutches of using fear to intimidate others. Your best people will honor you and embrace you for this. Then the strengths of others become your greatest ally, not your enemy.

Dose 79

There is no need at all to fear those who are better than you at certain tasks. This is the very reason that you need them and they need you. Therefore, shift your style of leading from fearful intimidation to open dialogue. Take the time to listen and understand those around you. Start with your family by apologizing for your closed style of communication. Ask them to pray for you to lead by humility and honesty.

Be open with those closest to you about your own fears and inadequacies. As you begin to share your fears, others will be given permission to do the same. Then something beautiful takes place. The walls of intimidation come tumbling down. People feel the freedom to fail and to be themselves. The home and work environments become places of encouragement and excellence. People's self-awareness is alive and well. Processes and people are constantly improving because there is total freedom to think of ways to do things better. Each of us is a candidate for being a genius in our own area of expertise.

A fearless culture incubates genius. By faith, extract fear from your home and work environments and replace it with freedom. This freedom of expression will silence intimidation!

God's Part

God encourages His children to boldly approach Him. His example encourages all leaders to become more approachable.

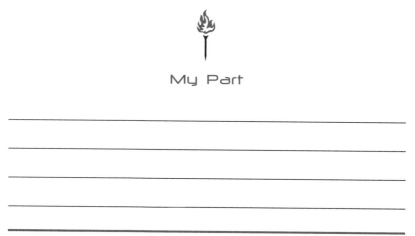

My Part

_____

_____

_____

_____

Hard Work

"...We worked night and day, laboring and toiling so that we would not be a burden to any of you. We did this, not because we did not have the right to such help, but in order to make ourselves a model for you to follow. For even when we were with you, we gave you this rule: 'If a man will not work, he shall not eat.'"
2 Thessalonians 3:8b-10

Hard work is honorable. It gives a man or woman respect for themselves and others. God is honored as well when you work hard. Be careful to not subscribe to a false theology that uses God in place of hard work. God, of course, is at work on our behalf but not without our sincere and focused efforts. However, it is much more than the simple "God helps those who help themselves" mentality. God has a grand design, and you are a part of His greater work. Your part is faithfulness and hard work. God's part is leading you into wise decisions, which produce the right results as He receives the glory.

As followers of Christ, the quality and quantity of our work is a reflection on God. Do not become the Christian whom everyone avoids because you are lazy and always make excuses. Be the Christian who is attractive because your work is excellent. People can depend on you, and you go the extra mile even when it is not your responsibility. For the good of the team and the glory of God you work hard. You may even deserve other benefits, but you refuse them during this season for the sake of the bigger picture.

Indeed, hard work keeps you out of trouble. When you are busy working hard, you do not have time to act badly. Gossip and complaining are absent from the lips of a hard worker. You simply do not have the time or energy to go there. It may be the sweat of your brow or the perspiration of your intellect; either way, work hard. Manual labor and mental toil both deserve hard work. Also, be careful to avoid being condescending toward others because their work role is different than yours. Blue collars need not bad mouth white collars, nor should white collars treat blue collars any less. We all need each other, and we all need to work hard.

Your hard work may produce wealth and abundance. Because of how society values your skills and services, you may even have an overabundance. Make sure you keep your success in perspective. Keep your heart tender toward God. We seem to pray more when we have little that when we have much more than we

Dose 80

need. Allow the fruit of your hard work to drive you to your knees in thanksgiving to God. Express your gratitude through generous giving. Hard work has its benefits; make sure to steward them well. Moreover, teach your children hard work. A child who is given everything can become soft on sin, discontent, demanding and ungrateful. Hard work teaches children the value of a dollar. It builds a discipline that will serve them throughout their lives. They learn how to work with and relate to people. Hard work is a must for a child to grow up into a healthy human being.

Lastly, keep your motive right as you work hard. Keep your focus off the money. Reward and compensation will come if the work is done with excellence. Stay the course working hard, loving your family and taking care of your health. Execute your hard work all for the glory of God. He is your boss. You are working for Him. Work hard. Work hard so that you can eat. Then you will be a blessing and not a burden to others!

God's Part

Hard work is not without reward: God sees, and God rewards those who labor for Him.

My Part

_____

_____

_____

_____

_____

Virtuous Woman

"A wife of noble character who can find? She is worth far more than rubies."
Proverbs 31:10

A woman of character is not easily found. She is rare and valuable. Because of her appealing attributes, she is a gift from God. Thank Him often if you are blessed with this quality of woman in your life. She is rare because we live in a self-crazed culture, yet a woman of character is others-focused. For the follower of Christ, selflessness is expected but, for our society as a whole, it is an anomaly. She refuses to demean herself to a standard of mediocrity. Her goal is excellence in living. Duplicity is far from her thinking as she serves with authenticity and industry. No skills or gifts remain dormant in her active life. She channels her energies into the welfare of her family and is resourceful with financial opportunities.

A woman of character is an anchor for her family. Your character provides stability when challenges creep into your home. You are determined to do the right thing regardless of the difficulties it may require. Character is more important than compromise, therefore you model the way for your friends and family. You are a rock of hope and consistency because God's Word has become that for you.

However, be careful to not take the world on your shoulders—that is God's job. Also do not hold a standard of perfection over your head. Leave yourself some wiggle room for mistakes. You will make mistakes. Let mistakes be a reminder of what to do and what not to do in the future. They are reminders of your dependence on God. Your goal is not to live a mistake-free life but a life that loves God and loves people. Let Him continue to develop your character and grow you into a mentor of other women. Don't waste your wonderful experiences. Share them with younger women so that they can grow in their character.

Husband, love your wife of character. Tell her often how proud you are of her. Do not be intimidated by her level of spirituality. On the contrary, celebrate her passion for life and her spiritual maturity. Allow her life to challenge you and inspire you to the same level of character development. Your virtuous woman is a tremendous asset. Your best and most strategic business decision occurred when you married a woman of character. Her wisdom is unparalleled. Her discernment of human nature borders on the divine. She is uncanny in seeing things you do

Dose 81

not see—and saving you a ton of money and time (that is if you listen to her). Her influence is ubiquitous in your work and home. Encourage her burgeoning influence and opportunities. Become her biggest cheerleader. If she wants to start a business, help her start a business. If she needs some help with the house and lawn, make that investment. Free her to do what she does best. It may be teaching, mentoring, being a mom, sewing or serving in a variety of capacities. It may be to take care of her parents during this stage of life.

Allow her to reach her full potential. Give her the cash, confidence and resources to reach for her dreams. Be grateful. A woman of character is not to be taken for granted. Yet this is easy to do. Make a big deal out of her accomplishments, because they are a big deal. Help her to pace herself and protect her from the encroachment of those with warped motives. Her character is a valued asset that needs to be managed with care. Care for her as she cares for you!

God's Part

A virtuous woman is a gift of God to her family.

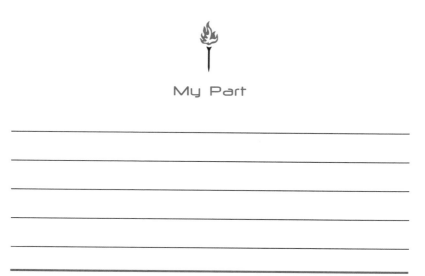

My Part

_____

_____

_____

_____

_____

Strength in God

"David was greatly distressed because the men were talking of stoning him;
each one was bitter in spirit because of his sons and daughters.
But David found strength in the Lord his God."
1 Samuel 30:6

God is your source of strength. Other sources will run dry, or
lose their effectiveness. Strength outside of God is temporary at best, and cannot
be depended upon. You may find strength for a while through your sheer deter-
mination and will power. But, eventually, your own efforts will dissipate in
power. A life striving in self-directed strength will expire without an ongoing
infusion of the Lord's strength. He is our life, yet we sometimes neglect our built-
in energy source.

Sheer busyness or fear may have caused you to unplug from your eternal
source of strength. Your faith need not remain impotent. Indeed, by faith you
can plug into the socket of your Savior Jesus. He has been there all the time.
Though your life may have been on an excursion away from eternal interests,
now is the time to reconnect with God. Do not allow the cares of this world to
choke out the hope you have in Christ. You can find strength in Him, without
having to look far at all. Sometimes we search for strength in all the wrong places
and then sheepishly come back to God. There is no need to circumvent Christ.
You can't improve on Jesus. Fall at His feet, and He will pick you up and fill you
with His power.

The power of God is unparalleled in conquering fear and discouragement.
You may have lost a loved one through death. Their influence in your life was
immense. You will miss them sorely. Their faith was a rock of reassurance for
you. But, now it is time to tap into the same strength that caused the faith of
your friend to flourish. When you dig down deep with the Lord, you do not
come away empty. He fills you to the brim, even to overflowing!

God is your burden-bearer and your strength-giver. Do not neglect to allow
His Spirit to ignite your strength to love. Ask Him to enlarge your heart of love,
so that He can love more through you. God takes your almost empty heart and
fills it fully with His strength. This is the paradox of His power: Your weakness
and emptiness means that you have depleted self and are now in position to be
fully filled by Him. Ironically, now you are in a position of strength.

Dose 82

This is how God works. He empties us of ourselves, so that He can fill us with Himself. So, your tentative and weak state is really to your advantage. Humility and even fear position you to be strengthened in the Lord. Therefore, stay low in the Lord. Moreover, He gives you strength so that you can do the same for others. Your newfound strength in Him is not meant to remain sterile—rather, it's meant to be viral.

Your strength in the Lord is for the sake of others. God's strength is meant to be unleashed. It is designed to serve the destiny of others. There are weak people all around you who are vulnerable to preying imposters of the faith. It is your authentic strength of character, residing in Christ, that is attractive to them. They discern this in you and desire to be strengthened by the Lord. So, allow them to lean on you for a time. Your being there for them is like a blood transfusion of God's strength. Their faith has become anemic through adversity, and God is using you to build up their eternal immunities. Strength in the Lord provides energy into eternity. Tap into it daily, for your sake and for the sake of others!

God's Part

God promises that a well of living water will spring up from within every believer, providing strength for living and strength for sharing.

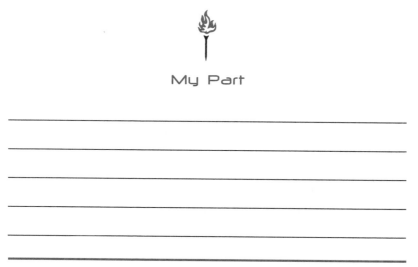

My Part

_____

_____

_____

_____

_____

He Cares

"Cast all your anxiety on him because he cares for you."
1 Peter 5:7

God cares about you. He cares about your job. He cares about your fears. He cares about your wife. He cares about your husband. He cares about your children. He cares about your parents. He cares about your worries. He cares about your finances. He cares about your car and your house. He also cares about your character. He cares about you caring about Him and caring for others. He is a caring God. You cannot out-care God. His capacity to care is infinite, and His competence to care is matchless. You can care because He cares. There is no care of yours that God does not care about. If it is important to you, then God cares about it.

Yes, you will experience misdirected cares. But God's desire is to come along side you and realign your cares with what He cares about the most. This is the beauty of your caring heavenly Father. He cares enough to bear your anxieties and to replace them with His peace and assurance. When you give God your worries, you in turn receive His calming presence. God's system of care is countercultural. God transforms your cares into what He cares about. However, there is one word of caution. Be careful and do not fall into the comparison trap. Your measurement on how to behave is not another person's measurement. We all have our struggles with sin and life. God has wired us all differently. Equally, spiritual people may cast their cares on God in polar opposite ways. One may find release in a quiet, written prayer, while another may feel cared for by God through lively worship. Let another's processing of anxiety be a guide and not a guilty comparison.

You know that God cares immensely, so how do you cast your cares on Him? By faith, you let Him care. It is all about trust. He cares and He can be trusted, therefore allow Him to do what He does best. You allow Him to care for you. This does take humility on your part. You are acknowledging a desperate need for God.

Your declaration of dependence is two-fold. First, you admit you are anxious and that you can't handle your worry alone. And second, you submit to the fact that only God can handle this level of concern. Hence, your submission to God allows His care to consume your anxieties. This is a process. Your care giving to

Dose 83

God is recurring. Over time He helps bring your feeble faith and misguided mind into focus on Him. What started as a burden, He transforms into a blessing. Pain becomes productive. You become free to care for others, because you have been freely cared for by Him. Your perspective takes on a heavenly flavor. Do not wait until matters get worse before you off-load your cares on God. Go to God first, because He cares the most. Let bad news travel fast, because He already knows. A carefree attitude is cultivated by resting in an all-caring God. The more you allow Him to care about your worries, the less you have to care. Then you can focus your cares on people and eternal issues.

Let God be consumed with your cares, so that you are not. Then you are positioned to care for others. You can lead others to your all-caring Christ. Care for them like Jesus. Your care will lead to His care. This is the beauty of the circle of care. You do it right, and they will want your God. You care for others, and they will want the God that cares for you. Keep your caring Christ-centered. You care because He cares. You can care because you have let Him care for you. Keep the circle of care rotating. Do not grow weary of caring. He doesn't. He cares for you. Therefore, give Him your cares and experience His care. He is your #1 caregiver!

God's Part

God is big enough to carry the cares of the world—literally.

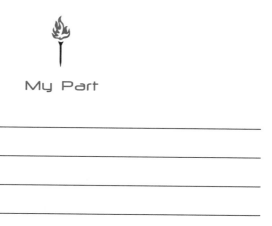

My Part

_____

_____

_____

_____

Pure Living

*"How can a young man keep his way pure? By living according
to your word."*
Psalm 119:9

God's Word is a filter for pure living. His Word extracts the
sediment of selfish living. It is a purifier. Without the purifying effect of the
Word, we become polluted in our thinking and distasteful with our words.
Everything about us becomes soiled by sin. Sin is dirty—it stains our lives. But,
the Word of God can remove sin's stains and clean us up. Clean living is the way
to go. It frees you from guilt and unshackles you from the complexities sin
creates. Adultery is complicated: It ravages relationships and pollutes some families for a lifetime. Lying is complicated: You have to remember and cover up
more than you are capable of covering. It is a messy web of deceit.

The same happens when any other areas of our lives are not kept clean.
Without proper physical hygiene we begin to smell, and there is a good chance
that we will contract an illness. Impure physical living is not healthy. Any
mechanical equipment, if left to itself, will operate less efficiently at best. If maintenance is chronically ignored, it will eventually shut down. The same is true for
our home or car. If either is cluttered with stuff, disorganized, and dirty, it
becomes a distraction. Both car and home left unclean are not pleasant places to
occupy. Left unattended and uncared for, they both deteriorate to junky and
trashy environments instead of the inviting environments they once were. Our
lives can follow this same downward spiral if they are not constantly cleansed by
God's Word. We need a daily "bath" in God's Word to prevent us from becoming
smelly to Him and others. We need to emit the pleasant aroma of righteousness
rather than the rank smell of sin. We need inviting lives.

The application of God's Word is the critical piece of pure living. You can
listen to it being taught and never change. You can talk about it and still remain
captive to bad habits and attitudes. You can even study it, memorize it and meditate on it, but allow it to feed your pride instead of your humility. Knowing and
understanding God's Word does not guarantee pure living. However these are
necessary steps. If humility and forgiveness are infiltrating your life more and
more, you know that you are on the right track. If the character of Christ is
engulfing your behavior more and more, you are on the road of purity. A pure
life means you are able to see God for who He is. He is high and lifted up, holy

Dose 84

and majestic. He is your heavenly Father, full of grace and compassion, waiting for you ever so patiently. God can be clearly distinguished through the lens of pure eyes. Purity does not mean perfection or some pseudo-spirituality. It means honesty in acknowledging your need to come clean with God and people. It is not hiding secret sins of lust and emotional attraction for someone other than your spouse. Purity is not slithering around in the dark corners of sin. Rather, purity results as you "sunbathe" in the bright rays of accountability. People know your defects and your strengths. There are no surprises. You are real and receptive to the correction, teaching, and even the rebuke of God and others. Purity implies the removal of impurities. This may or may not be an easy process. However, if purity is exercised consistently, impurity buildup is minimal. If the buildup is minimal, then the shame and embarrassment of unclean living can be kept at bay.

Both young and old can enjoy pure living. Like taking a hot shower after a hard day's work in the yard, you become refreshed and revitalized. You smell sweet, and people are attracted to your life. Pure living is fueled by the Word of God, so learn it and live it!

God's Part

God turns on the pure light of His Word and shines it into the dark crevices of our lives—exposing impure, sinful aspects, and providing tools and grace to remove them.

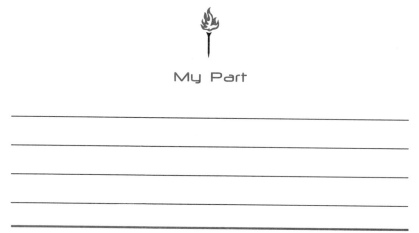

My Part

_____

_____

_____

_____

_____

False Security

"When the soldiers returned to the camp, the elders of Israel asked,
'Why did the Lord bring defeat upon us today before the Philistines?
Let us bring the ark of the Lord's covenant from Shiloh, so that it may
go with us and save us from the hand of our enemies.'"
1 Samuel 4:3

Our security is in God alone. Security is not found in a representation of God, but in God. The church is the bride of Christ, but it is not your security. Your spouse is your lifelong companion, but he or she is not your security. Money is useful, but it is not your security. Your children are a blessing, but they are not your security. Your job is necessary, but it is not your security. Armies protect nations, but national security is ultimately God's call. God does not allow the security that only comes from Him to be found in another. This is why He is God.

He is the secure one. You are eternally secure in Christ. Do not fret over your fearful situation. Rather, seek your security in Christ. You will become insecure if you attempt to be secure outside of Jesus. There is not enough money, time or insulation from the world that can keep you secure, only Christ can do that. Security is His prerogative. Any substitute for His security is an attempt to prostitute His peace. It can't be done.

Security is not found in Jesus plus something else. This only dilutes the security of your Savior. Do not spend all your effort and energy arranging a secure life. You will never be satisfied with your self-made security. Authentic security and contentment are in the Lord. He is your security guard. As you follow Him, anything in your life has to come through His care. However, for better or for worse He does not allow us to live in a risk-free environment. Yes, we have freedom in Christ but not without danger. Tragedy could strike any day. A car accident, a terminal illness, a rebellious child, a lost job, or rejection from a friend can shake your confident security in the Lord.

So, when your faith is tested, will you still rely on His stellar track record of security? Or, will you panic and make matters worse by relaxing your principles or even abandoning your faith in God? Now is not the time to bail on God. You are still secure in Him, even when things go wrong. Do not choose to battle through life alone. You will lose if you do. You will lose sleep—maybe your health, peace and security. Stay true to heaven's security forces. His angels are

Dose 85

sentries of care who watch over you. A spiritual battle is raging all around you. Satan will crush your self-made security, but he flees in the face of a man or woman secure in Christ. There are no weapons in his arsenal that can penetrate the solid armor of God. The armor of the Lord defines His attributes of security. Your freedom is secured by His belt of truth. Your heart is protected by His breastplate of righteousness. You can walk securely with Him, because your feet are covered by His peace. You can be confident that His shield of faith extinguishes the fiery arrows of the enemy. Your mind is secured by His helmet of salvation.

Your offensive security lies in the sword of the Spirit, which is the Word of God. Now this is security "up close and personal." Chose each day to be suited up by the Lord, and you will be secure. An exposed life is an insecure life. Therefore, be clothed with Christ. Security is in your Savior alone!

God's Part

The Lord alone provides true security. He Himself is our rock, our sure foundation, our strong tower, our mighty defender.

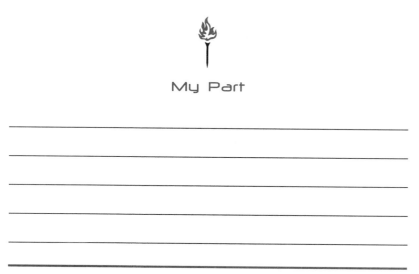

My Part

_____

_____

_____

_____

_____

Patient Endurance

"…This calls for patient endurance and faithfulness on the part of the saints."
Revelation 13:10b

Patient endurance is not easy, but many times it is necessary. If you change jobs every two years ten times in a row, you do not have twenty years of work experience. You have two years of work experience in ten different places. So, make sure that you learn what God intends for you to learn where you are before you move on.

This is one of Satan's ploys. His desire is to keep you reactive to life, accompanied by a shallow faith. Your faith has the opportunity to go deep when you stay somewhere for a while, but your faith remains shallow when you run from resistance. Resistance is a faith builder. When you are pressed against by life (what sometimes seems from all sides), you have the opportunity for growth. This is where patient endurance can serve you well. Patient endurance says that I will stay in this marriage, because it is for better or for worse. I will allow God to change me for the better, and I will trust Him to do the same for my spouse over time.

Indeed, patient endurance is able to outwait and sometimes outlive its accusers. Accusers come and go. If they do not get the reaction or desired response from you, then they will move on to other unprotected prey. So, by faith, "out-endure" your enemies. There will always be someone who does not like you. Don't think you can appease everyone; this is not possible or healthy. Appeasement may grant concessions that come back to haunt you. It is one thing to negotiate with those who represent a spirit of good will. It is a whole other deal to compromise with someone who is totally at odds with your values and principles. Be willing to walk away. It is not worth it to do business with an enraged enemy.

Patient endurance is illustrated throughout the Bible. Jesus patiently endured the cross. He patiently endured His critics and, ultimately, He more than restored His reputation when He proved His claims by His resurrected life. David patiently endured the fallout from his adultery and murder. He had pushed himself to the point of totally turning his back on God but, instead, he turned back to God and became a broken and humbled leader. Joseph patiently endured

"He who walks with the wise grows wise, but a companion of fools suffers harm." Proverbs 13:20

Dose 86

the ridicule and jealousy of family members. Their injustice drove his faith in God deeper and broader. His patient endurance during the horrific injustice of his imprisonment led to his godly influence over a kingdom. Hannah patiently endured her inability to bear children. Her faithfulness to God during barrenness was a testimony of encouragement to friends, family and a nation. Her womb was empty, but her faith was pregnant with God possibilities.

Therefore, do not be tempted to take the easy way out. The easy way, many times, is not the best way. Yes, there is a time to cut your losses, but only after you have patiently endured and exhausted your options. People are watching how you "do life." So, use your influence to help others patiently endure their situations. Faithfulness, when you don't feel like it, is evidence of a maturing faith. You may be on the verge of experiencing God's very best. However, do not confuse procrastination with patient endurance. Patient endurance is active and productive. It is not misguided, apathetic or irresponsible waiting. It is daily depending on and seeking God for His best.

Therefore, patiently endure for God's sake and for the sake of others. Heavenly rewards await those who patiently endure. Moreover, your faith will never be the same!

God's Part

Jesus patiently endured the cross, despising its shame, for the glory that was to follow.

My Part

_____

_____

_____

_____

_____

Heavenly Help

"I lift up my eyes to the hills—where does my help come from? My help comes from the Lord, the Maker of heaven and earth."
Psalm 121:1-2

It's OK to ask for help. In fact many times help is needed by you and expected by God. Your heavenly Father desires deeply to help His children. He can't wait to be there for you. But, to benefit from the help of God, we have to look up. We look up from the mess and mire of our circumstances and see God extend His comfort and security. We look up from our financial debacle and hear God say, "Don't worry, I will provide for you." We look up from our relational quagmire, and God pours out His forgiveness and longs for a deeper and more intimate relationship with us.

We can and should do the same for others. When we look up out of our prosperity and see that God is there, it helps us remain grateful and generous with His blessing. Heavenly help starts by looking up and recognizing that almighty God is available, seated in glory, awaiting our engagement. He is the creator of the galaxies, yet He is ever ready to help you. Nothing is too small or insignificant for the compassion of God. He cares about His creation. He is responsible as your creator for your well-being. He wants to help. He wants to provide peace where there is turmoil. His presence is calming when there is chaos. His Holy Spirit is your helper. He will lead, convict and comfort you all at the same time. There are no capacity issues with the Holy Spirit. He is 100% involved at all times for the followers of Jesus Christ. It is simply a matter of our tapping into His tremendous resources. Look up before it is too late. Look up while He can still be found. Heaven is waiting to help.

God has divine insomnia. He never sleeps or slumbers. He is always there to listen and guide you. His "help desk" is open 24/7. Imagine calling on God in the middle of the night. The midnight call to God does not encounter a prolonged ring, a disgruntled customer service representative or voice mail. Your 911 call to God receives the calm and loving assurance of your heavenly Father immediately.

He is available and yearns to help in any way He can. Just as every good parent wants to help his child, so does your heavenly Father—times ten. Moms and dads are the first to administer medicine to their sick children, defend their

Dose 87

disenfranchised son or daughter or celebrate their accomplishments. They are there to help.

This is a reminder not to discount God's earthly help agents. The Body of Christ is available to help you. You have helped others all these years, and now you are in a stage of great need. Do not allow your pride to keep you quiet. Your brothers and sisters of faith need to understand your fate. You are hypocritical to put on the guise of normalcy when all hell is breaking loose in your life. It actually is a great encouragement to your caregivers to understand that their helper has needs too.

You are not immune to the help of people. In fact, your availability for help will bless others in ways that you cannot imagine. Let God help first and let His children help second. It is a divine process that rallies the troops in heaven and on earth. You are not alone. Allow help to minister to you, and one day you will do the same. Help is on the way!

God's Part

Any help we ever receive ultimately comes from the hand of God.

My Part

_____

_____

_____

_____

_____

Distractions Divide

"As Saul and his forces were closing in on David and his men to capture them, a messenger came to Saul, saying, 'Come quickly! The Philistines are raiding the land.' Then Saul broke off his pursuit of David and went to meet the Philistines. This is why they call this place Sela Hammahlekoth."
I Samuel 23:26b-28

Distractions—good or bad—can get you off track.

This is the nature of a distraction. It causes you to become double minded. You are unable to give full attention to the matter at hand, and thus you water down your effectiveness. It may be a personal or a professional distraction that currently has you preoccupied.

Personally, it may be a relationship that is sucking an inordinate amount of time and energy. Is it really worth it? The hours of "high maintenance" relational care may mean that it's not meant to be. The attention to this individual has become laborious and highly intense. Without any relief in sight, it may be time to walk away for a season. Let it rest until there can be more normalcy to the relationship. For example, a person's drug, alcohol or sexual addiction needs professional attention. Your tolerance is only enabling their bad behavior. They are distracting you from being the parent, or the spouse, God intended you to be. Their destructive behavior requires tough love. Otherwise, you may lose everything in the process. Do not allow someone's premeditated distraction to lead your family into destruction. It may be time for bold intervention.

On the other hand, you may be experiencing a professional distraction. The mission of your organization may be compromised because of your well-meaning activities outside the scope of your job description. Do an audit of your time and energy. Be honest with yourself. Either you must cease feeding your distractions by aligning your personal and professional missions, or you are choosing to jeopardize the integrity and success of both initiatives.

Indeed, our worst outcome from distractions is the neglect of our time with our heavenly Father. He deserves our full attention and focus. If life has become too busy for God, then we are too busy. There is no distraction worth sacrificing our time with the Lord. It may even be that your service for God has become a distraction. Ironically, you cannot spend time with God, because you are serving God. This is a great deception. Service for God, which substitutes activity for

Dose 88

your time with God, is a distraction of the worst kind. You drift into a perform-ance-based relationship with your heavenly Father which is full of pressure and missed expectations. You are distracted by doing and have no margin for being. You are unable to know Him because you are too busy working for Him. It may be time to modify your doing so that you can take time for being. Be loved by God. Be accepted by God. Be encouraged by God. Be led by God.

A distracted life is susceptible to imbalance. Remove those "good" distrac-tions, and replace them with intimacy with God. He will make up for any lost time and even accomplish more in your absence. Distractions can divide us from our Maker. Therefore, defuse distractions before they arrive. Then you are posi-tioned to be united with your Lord. By His grace, push back on distraction's pull!

God's Part

Although He made time to touch the needs of multitudes, Jesus never allowed the pressing crowd to divert His focus from His primary mission or from communion with His Father.

My Part

_____

_____

_____

_____

_____

_____

Call for Wisdom

"This calls for wisdom."
Revelation 13:18a

Wisdom is required more often than we realize. It is wisdom that cuts through emotion and gets to the reality of the situation. "What is the wise thing to do?" is an effective question in decision making. "What is best for the enterprise?" is a wise question to ask as it relates to business and ministry. And, many times, God speaks through money—or the lack thereof. So, if money is tight, then we need to be extremely wise with expenditures. Wisdom says to cut back on expenses and do not add additional costs. At this point it is not about lack of faith, it is about being a wise steward with what you have so that you can be trusted with more. Wise stewardship attracts generous givers.

Another characteristic of wisdom is that it is neither impatient nor desperate. Wisdom takes a step back and thoroughly evaluates a situation before charging ahead. For instance, your child has been accepted simultaneously into a state college, and an out-of-state college. By attending the in-state school the first year, you have the option to save and pay cash for the out-of-state tuition the following year. You are wise when you take opportunities like this to avoid debt. Harmless debt today many times becomes unwise debt tomorrow.

So, are you soliciting wisdom on a consistent basis? Knowledge and experience mixed with common sense and discernment is a great recipe for wisdom. Wisdom is seeking to understand God's perspective on matters. This is why the wisdom found in God's Word is so relevant for living. The Bible is a treasure trove of wisdom waiting to be discovered by the wise wisdom hunter. Seek out wisdom, and you will find something more valuable than money or possessions. Any fool can stumble into money, but only the wise can retain riches. Wisdom sits under our nose waiting to be tapped.

Therefore, not only pray, read and meditate on the Bible, but also seek out the wise. Look for people with gray in their hair and who exhibit wise behavior. The wise will help you validate the inklings of wisdom you are beginning to grasp from your study of Scripture. Read books and listen to messages from men and women who are wise. Try to daily expose your mind and heart to sources of wisdom. Hang out long enough with wisdom, and it will rub off on you. So, take every opportunity to call on wisdom. Be wise in your relationships. Be wise

"He who walks with the wise grows wise, but a companion of fools suffers harm." Proverbs 13:20

Dose 89

with your money. Be wise with your time. Before you realize it, your wisdom will attract others who are hungry for the same. Moreover, the crown jewel of wisdom accumulation may be the fear of the Lord. *"The fear of the Lord is the beginning of knowledge, but fools despise wisdom and discipline"* (Proverbs 1:7). The fear of God positions you to receive wisdom. No fear of God means no wisdom. No wonder our world is flush with fools! We have lost our fear of God, and thus wisdom has alluded us. The fear of the Lord is an incubator for wisdom. God dispenses wisdom to those who fear Him. Therefore, love God, but fear Him. Worship God, but fear Him. Learn of God, but fear Him. Serve God, but fear Him. Your fear of God qualifies you for wisdom. Do not become so familiar with God that you lose your fear of God. This is unwise and leads to foolishness.

Wisdom awaits your harvest call. Pluck it and enjoy it, like plump, luscious and juicy fruit on a hot summer day. Taste and see that wisdom is good. No one has ever complained of attaining too much wisdom. Call on wisdom often. Seek out the wise, and ask them and God for wisdom. This is the wise thing to do!

God's Part

God is the source of all wisdom, and He promises to give it to all who ask Him.

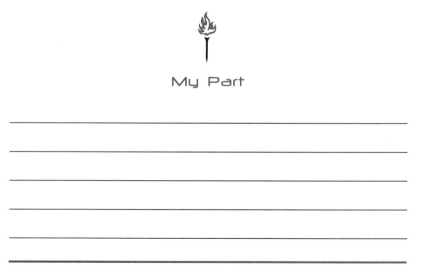

My Part

_____

_____

_____

_____

_____

⊔od Audit

"Search me, O God, and know my heart; test me and know my anxious thoughts. See if there is any offensive way in me, and lead me in the way everlasting."
Psalm 139:23-24

Expect God to conduct a regular audit of our lives. His Holy Spirit is an expert at probing beneath the surface of our actions and is able to root out unhealthy motives and habits. God's accountability is thorough and swift. He is honest, steadfast and unbiased. I can talk myself into anything, but God holds my feet to the fire of His expectations. He searches your heart looking for payouts of forgiveness to others. Your books do not need to be loaded up with accounts receivable that hang over others like a bad dream. God will deal with their shortcomings and the pain they have inflicted. Keep your accounts short. You have the ability in Christ to forgive others of their debt. Write off their offenses and you will build up your heavenly tax credits.

This is what we do as Christians. We forgive. We forgive because of the great mercy we have received from our heavenly Father. Another common discovery from God's audit is fear. Our minds swirl with scenarios out of our control. Fear of failure, fear of confrontation, fear of rejection and fear of what might happen can immobilize you. These fears birth anxious thoughts that refuse to go away. They race back and forth through your head uncontrollably. God's probing will put a finger on your worries, and He will remind you to trust Him. He gently and lovingly says not to let anxiety drive you but to trust instead. He can handle whatever He uncovers in your life, and He can handle whatever you encounter in life. This is what He does as God. He is the calmer during uncertainty and the stabilizer when you face difficult circumstances. This is where you trust your heavenly auditor. You trust God that whatever He asks you to change will be for your good and the good of others. His audit is for your benefit since He already knows His conclusions before He starts.

However this divine accounting of our life is based on an invitation. Yes, God does have His Holy Spirit performing an internal audit at all times. As a follower of Jesus Christ you can never get away from His prompting, His convicting and His comfort. He is ever at work even when you are unaware. But, busyness can barricade you from the Holy Spirit's influence. You can run so hard that you run right by His warning signs. Your wife says to slow down, you are

Dose 90

missing the children growing up, but you keep running—before you know it they are moving out bound to college. Your body screams to slow down, but you keep running—until your first heart attack. Your schedule says to slow down but you keep running while, in the process, you are breaking promises and letting people down. A "God audit" means that you may need to go away and open up the books of your life to the life-giver Himself. This is a good place to begin trusting that things will go just fine as you take the time to listen to your heavenly auditor. His laws are not complicated, though we have a tendency to complicate them. Listen intently and obey.

Once your God audit is complete, painful as it may be, He is ready to lead you forward with His game plan. This pause in your schedule is meant to propel you forward. Your introspection, confession and repentance free you to move forward in the power of the Holy Spirit. This is the genius of a divine audit. Your freedom and opportunities explode now that you are God compliant. Clean books and a clear conscience expand your capacity. Now you are energized for God's next assignment. Schedule your God audit today!

God's Part

The audits that God conducts in our lives are continuous. However, it's at our invitation that He allows us a glimpse at His books. Repentance, forgiveness and reconciliation put everything right again.

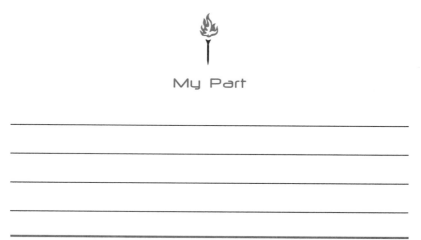

My Part

_____

_____

_____

_____

_____

Index of Biblical References

The Good Samaritans

"She opens her arms to the poor and extends her hands to the needy."
Proverbs 31:20

Boyd, his daughter Bethany (R) and her friend Ali Ibsen (L) serving the poor with Ananthi in the slums of New Delhi

Ananthi Jebasingh is a modern-day Mother Teresa. No one I know of is serving, educating and sharing the love of Jesus with the poorest of the poor like Ananthi. Please prayerfully consider supporting the Good Samaritan School in New Delhi, India with your prayers and financial support. *"Jesus said, 'Let the little children come to me, and do not hinder them, for the kingdom of heaven belongs to such as these.'"* (Matthew 19:14)

Boyd Bailey

.

www.FriendsoftheGoodSamaritans.org

About the Author

Boyd Lee Bailey is cofounder and Chief Executive Officer of Ministry Ventures, a non-profit incubator and accelerator for ministries. Founded in 2000, Ministry Ventures has helped 25 new ministries raise over 7.5 million dollars and impact over 35,000 people for Christ. He is also founder and Chairman of Wisdom Hunters, LLC. Boyd and his wife Rita live in Roswell, Georgia. They have been married 27 years and are blessed with four daughters and two sons-in-law who love Jesus! Prior to Ministry Ventures, Boyd was the National Director for Crown Financial Ministries. He was instrumental in the expansion of Crown into 30 major markets across the U.S. He was a key facilitator in the 25 million dollar merger between Christian Financial Concepts and Crown Ministries. Before Crown, he and Andy Stanley started First Baptist Atlanta's north campus; and as an Elder, Boyd assisted Andy in the start of North Point Community Church.

Boyd Bailey was born in Huntsville, Alabama and received his Bachelor of Arts from Jacksonville State University and his Masters of Divinity from Southwestern Seminary in Fort Worth, Texas. In college he bought a service business with five employees. This business endeavor financed his education and the equity from its sale was the economic launching pad for his graduate school experience.

Boyd serves on the boards of Ministry Ventures, The Infocus Group, Wisdom Hunters, Treasures, Light in the Darkness and Friends of the Good Samaritans. He is engaged in a mentor program with 10 other younger business and ministry leaders, and he and Rita lead a couple's community group in their home. Bailey has co-authored a small group curriculum, written several articles and just completed his first two books, *Launch* and *Infusion*.

His hobbies and interests include history, reading and research, investments, leisure travel, speaking, sports, movies, running, the outdoors and his greatest passion—hanging out with his family!

"He who walks with the wise grows wise, but a companion of fools suffers harm." Proverbs 13:20